# WORLD FILM LOCATIONS TOKYO

Edited by Chris MaGee

First Published in the UK in 2011 by Intellect Books, The Mill, Parnall Road, Fishponds, Bristol, BS16 3JG, UK

First Published in the USA in 2011 by Intellect Books, The University of Chicago Press, 1427 E. 60th Street, Chicago, IL 60637, USA

Copyright ©2011 Intellect Ltd

Cover Image: Anonymous Content/ Dune Films

Copy Editor: Emma Rhys

Intern Support: George Murkin, Judith Pearson, Carly Spencer and Hannah Evans

A Catalogue record for this book is available from the British Library

**World Film Locations Series**
ISSN: 2045-9009
eISSN: 2045-9017

**World Film Locations Tokyo**
ISBN: 978-1-84150-483-4
eISBN: 978-1-84150-531-2

Printed and bound by Bell & Bain Limited, Glasgow

# WORLD FILM LOCATIONS
## TOKYO

EDITOR
Chris MaGee

SERIES EDITOR & DESIGN
Gabriel Solomons

DESIGN ASSISTANT
Persephone Coelho

CONTRIBUTORS
Jacopo Francesco Acqua
Mateo Boscarol
John Berra
Eric Evans
Jason Gray
Matthew Hardstaff
James Heron
Brandon Hocura
Naomi Hocura
Catherine Monroe Hotes
Samuel Jamier
Jon Jung
Chris MaGee
Tom Mes
Maria Roberta Novielli
Marc Sint-Cyr
Stephen Sarrazin
Reiko Tahara

PUBLISHED BY
Intellect
The Mill, Parnall Road,
Fishponds, Bristol, BS16 3JG. UK
T: +44 (0) 117 9589910
F: +44 (0) 117 9589911
E: info@intellectbooks.com

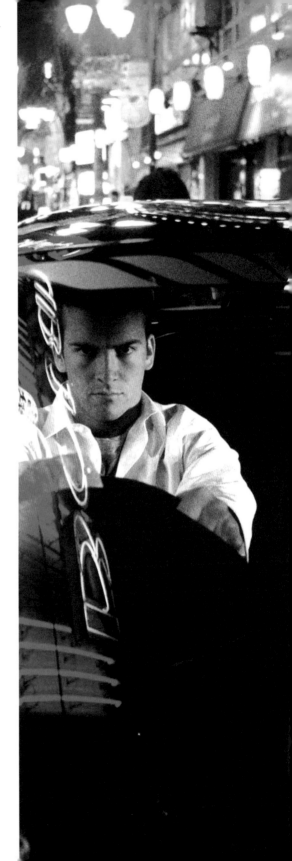

# CONTENTS

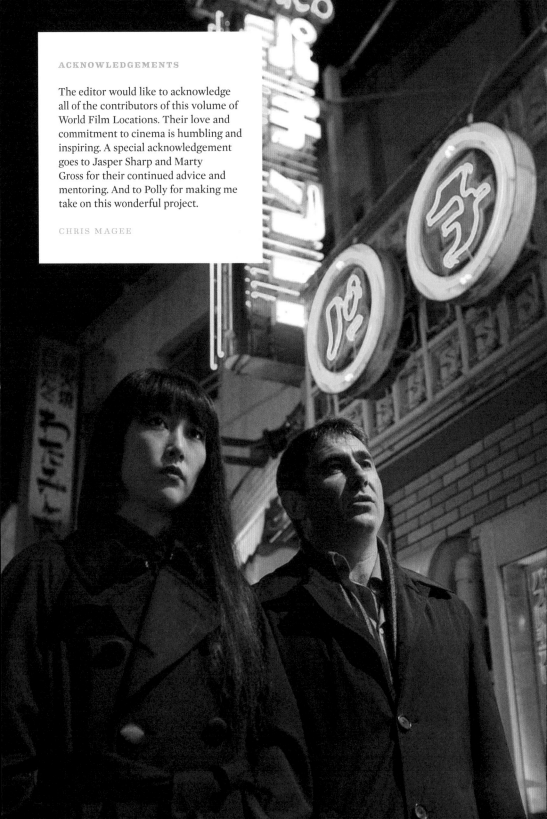

ACKNOWLEDGEMENTS

The editor would like to acknowledge
all of the contributors of this volume of
World Film Locations. Their love and
commitment to cinema is humbling and
inspiring. A special acknowledgement
goes to Jasper Sharp and Marty
Gross for their continued advice and
mentoring. And to Polly for making me
take on this wonderful project.

CHRIS MAGEE

# INTRODUCTION

**World Film Locations** *Tokyo*

**CITIES ARE CAST IN FILMS** in much the same way casting directors hire actors. Each have their own unique characters that have been refined in the popular imagination by their repeated appearances in the movies. Exploring the world's great cities through film is exactly what the World Film Location series is about, and the volume you are holding right now is your guide to one of the most vibrant, ancient, and storied cities on the globe – Tokyo.

As you read through the 45 scenes reviewed in these pages, as well as the series of specially commissioned spotlight articles, you'll be able to begin to scratch the surface of a city that is both enlightening and misunderstood. Take heart, though, that you've got some of the best qualified tour guides for this journey. The World Film Locations series, and the Tokyo volume in particular, has brought together some of the most respected film experts to open the doors and peek into corners of places you may never have heard of; but the very best guides to Tokyo are the film-makers themselves.

For western film-makers Tokyo represents an interesting dichotomy of centuries-old traditions and cutting edge futurism, a world alien and yet strangely familiar where travellers are not only forced to transition from one culture to another, but often find themselves transitioning on a deeper personal level as well. You will find films like these here – *Lost in Translation* (Sophia Coppola, 2003) and *Enlightenment Guaranteed* (Doris Dörrie, 1999), amongst many others.

While film-makers from outside Japan have depicted Tokyo as a neon otherworld, Japanese film-makers have given us a totally different interpretation of their nation's capital. Tokyo represents the best of Japan, a nation's dream, in such classics as Yasujiro Ozu's *Tokyo Story*, Yoji Yamada's *Tora-san: It's Tough Being a Man* and Takashi Yamazaki's *Always: Sunset on Third Street*. Every dream has its flipside nightmare though and Tokyo can often be the vessel for Japanese film-makers to voice their grievances about living as part of Japan's hive society. Moments from such films as Kinji Fukasaku's *If You Were Young: Rage*, Hirokazu Koreeda's *Nobody Knows* and Gen Takahashi's *Confessions of a Dog* will introduce you to aspects of Tokyo that may make you flinch.

Tokyo is a big enough city and certainly a big enough idea that film-makers, whether foreign or native born, can view this unique metropolis from any umpteenth amount of angles. I must stress that these scenes are just a sampling of Tokyo's star turns on-screen. There are hundreds more out there for film lovers and nascent Japanophiles to discover. Hopefully this volume of World Film Locations will be a gateway to hours of movie watching and I can only hope a few round trip flights to Japan's capital city. ✣

**Chris MaGee, Editor**

# TOKYO

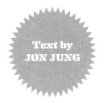

Text by
JON JUNG

*City of the Imagination*

'Tokyo is a city criss-crossed by trains, tied together with electric wire, she shows her veins' – *Sans Soleil, 1983*

**IN THE MANY URBAN SCENES** in *Blade Runner* (Ridley Scott, 1982), the audience is compelled to identify with a world that seems alien yet so familiar. Through dialogue and landmarks we discover that Ridley Scott's dystopic cops-and-replicants tale is set in Los Angeles, but there's no mistaking the influence that the Shinjuku and Ginza nightscapes have on the visual design of that film. That a few flashing neon signs over a night-time cityscape can evoke such association over visually similar cities such as Hong Kong and New York really exemplify Tokyo as the city of the imagination.

To call Tokyo a 'city' of the imagination, however, is a bit of a misnomer. Geographically speaking, Tokyo is not actually just a city, but a sprawling megalopolis which consists of the 23 wards that make up central Tokyo, 26 cities residing in its west, and

its many natural and artificial islands in its bay and surrounding ocean. The beauty of Tokyo lies in this balance: Central Tokyo, every bit the image of the metropolis in all its brash candy-colour glory, with the cattle-like droves of people and traffic, darting trains and massive skyscrapers shown in films like *Enter the Void* (Gaspar Noe, 2009) and *The Fast and The Furious: Tokyo Drift* (Justin Lin, 2006). Western Tokyo, built as the bedroom community of Tokyo's center, is generally the quiet and much more sane suburbs as depicted in *Adrift in Tokyo* (Satoshi Miki, 2007) and *Kakera* (Momoko Ando, 2009). Finally, the peaceful and austere islands, popular places of destination and playlands for traveling Tokyoites, can be seen in films such as *Battle Royale* (Kinji Fukasaku, 2000) and *Gojira/Godzilla* (Ishirô Honda, 1954), never mind all of the chaos and mayhem taking place around the beautiful scenery in those films. Tokyo as a destination or place to live has a lot going for it.

But Tokyo has been more than just a location. It's a brand, a fashion, a style, a flavour, a dream, and a wish. In 2010, the Japanese government, through its Ministry of Economy, Trade and Industry, developed a policy of 'Cool Japan' to help promote tourism and trade through its unique popular culture. A 'Cool Japan' office has even been set up within the Ministry and the policy itself is designed along the government's 'new growth strategy'. As well, a 'Cool Japan' TV show is broadcast on the cable arm of Japan's public network, NHK. According to the show's website, their goal, not surprisingly, is to '[illustrate] the quickly changing Japanese culture and how it is perceived by

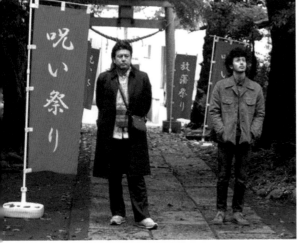

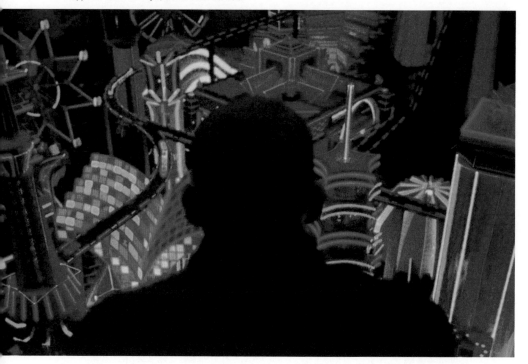

the international community.' Though some might question the policy's worth and timeliness; i.e. fans of Japan have been partaking of Japan's 'cool' for years; that the government acknowledges a facet of its society sparked solely in the imagination (coupled with a little product-driven capitalism) is almost a validation of Tokyo as a centre of the pop culture mecca. For what is 'Cool Japan' without the content creation of modern Japan; i.e. the fashion, anime, music, manga and technology, many of which are produced in Tokyo?

What's more, Tokyo has been more than just the city of the imagination in Japan; it's really been the city of the imagination for all of Asia. Tokyo has long been the symbol of the un-West, the place you go for that taste of Japan and Asia without the in-

**Tokyo has been more than just a location. It's a brand, a fashion, a style, a flavour, a dream, and a wish.**

conveniences of abandoning that (English language) newspaper and (French-brewed) coffee in the morning. A glance out the hotel window will reveal an urban sprawl, a depressing eruption of concrete buildings seemingly blotting out the beautiful nature for which Japan has become to be known. However, a walk through the actual city will reveal pockets of interest. A turn to the left might reveal a large, beautiful park with billowing cherry blossom trees in full bloom, a turn to the right and there may be a giant loud, flashy pachinko parlor. Walk up the street there may be a melancholic *obon* dance happening at the local temple, down the street, there may be a B-Boy dance battle happening in front of the station. Tokyo has literally become a 'what's your flavour' type of city, not just merely an East-meets-West paradigm, but a city of true cultural globalization and a place that begs to be looked at even more closely by the camera's lens.

Tokyo is the most exciting place to be because it is constantly changing. Want to know what's happening in Tokyo next? Just take a look up on the big screen and find out. ✤

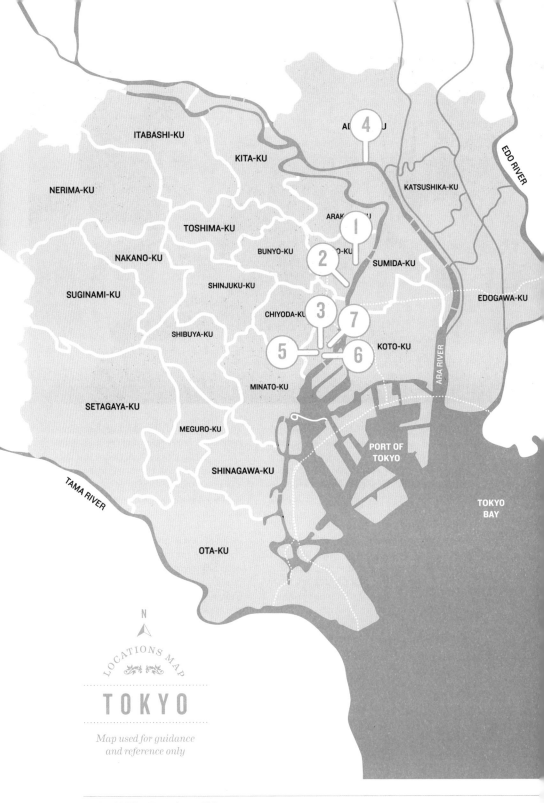

ITABASHI-KU

KITA-KU

NERIMA-KU

TOSHIMA-KU

NAKANO-KU

BUNYO-KU

SHINJUKU-KU

SUGINAMI-KU

SHIBUYA-KU

CHIYODA-KU

SETAGAYA-KU

MEGURO-KU

MINATO-KU

SHINAGAWA-KU

OTA-KU

AD____U    4

KATSUSHIKA-KU

EDO RIVER

ARAK____U    1

__O-KU    2    SUMIDA-KU

EDOGAWA-KU

3    7

5    6    KOTO-KU

ARA RIVER

PORT OF
TOKYO

TOKYO
BAY

TAMA RIVER

N

LOCATIONS MAP

TOKYO

Map used for guidance
and reference only

# TOKYO LOCATIONS

## SCENES 1-7

# TOKYO MARCH (1929)

*The most modernized city of the East*

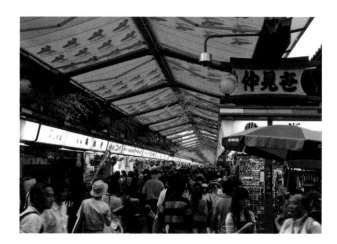

**IT'S A MIRACLE THAT WE CAN** enjoy films of Tokyo made before 1945. Not only was the actual nitrate-based film stock used before then fragile and highly flammable, but Tokyo itself suffered terribly during the first half of the twentieth century. The Great Kanto Earthquake of 1923 and the US-lead fire bombings of World War II would topple and pummel the Japanese capital. Once the Occupation began in the fall of 1945 many film prints that didn't burn in the bombing were deemed a threat to Japan's nascent democracy and ended up burning on the bonfires of US censors. These tragic events make the opening of Kenji Mizoguchi's *Tokyo March* that much more miraculous. Only 28 minutes survive of this melodrama about a beautiful geisha named Orie who comes between two friends, Yoshiki and Sakuma, but the first two minutes affords us a rare glimpse of pre-war Tokyo. We see the city through the wind shield of a speeding automobile: commuters run to catch a streetcar, patent leather shoes walk beside traditional geta, housewives, businessmen and bicyclists jockey in the street. Art deco-inspired inter-titles speak of 'the most modernized city of the East' and the vast metropolis' various districts – the 'chic town of Asakusa', 'the ever-changing Shinjuku' and Musashino where the moon 'shines over the rooftop of the shopping mall'. These fleeting, grainy shots of Tokyo are made all the more poignant by the fact that just sixteen years later the city would be almost totally destroyed in the war. ↝*Chris MaGee*

**Above** Nakamise shopping street, Sensoji Temple, Asakusa (Photo ©Richard Ryer)

*Directed by Kenji Mizoguchi*
*Timecode for scene: Pre-war Asakusa/Shinjuku/Musashino*
*Scene duration: 0:01:24 – 0:03:17*

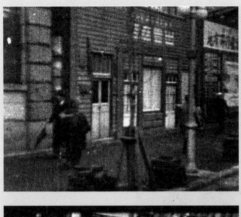
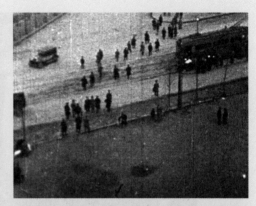
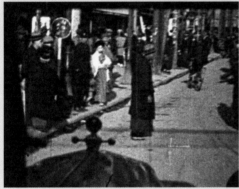
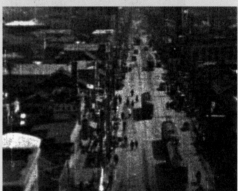

# STRAY DOG/NORA INU (1949)

LOCATION  *4 Ueno, Taito-ku, Ameyokocho*

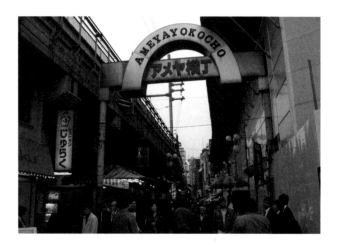

**PRESENT DAY AMEYOKOCHO** is a major shopping area which literally translates as 'American Alley' and is famous for the range of goods on offer from both department stores and market stalls. In the late-1940s, however, Ameyokocho was a thriving black market community, known for trading under-the-table American products, hence its significance to the plot of Akira Kurosawa's classic police procedural *Stray Dog*. When his gun is stolen while travelling on a crowded bus, disgraced Detective Murakami (Toshiro Mifune) becomes determined to restore his reputation by retrieving the weapon from the clutches of the criminal underworld. Murakami's self-assigned mission takes him to Ameyokocho where, disguised as an unkempt ex-soldier, he wanders around, attempting to establish the necessary lead. This lengthy sequence was shot by second unit director Ishiro Honda, who hid his handheld camera in a box as a means of capturing footage of Tokyo's seedy underbelly that would work within Kurosawa's film noir framework. Starting at Ueno station, Murakami makes his way through bars, brothels, flophouses and street markets, sweating under the sweltering sun, eventually making contact with a bandaged gangster while recuperating by a bombed-out fountain. If the undercover Murakami is looking for redemption, everyone else in Ameyokocho is simply seeking survival; Kurosawa superimposes Murakami's searching eyes over the crowded environment to show his realization that this is a world driven by desperation and populated by bottom-feeders. Ameyokocho burned down in late 1949, making this sequence a valuable record of the social collapse that constituted Japan's post-war underground economy. **John Berra**

**Above** Ameyokocho shopping street

*Directed by Akira Kurosawa*
**Scene description: Detective Murakami undercover at the black market**
*Timecode for scene: 0:18:18 – 0:29:37*

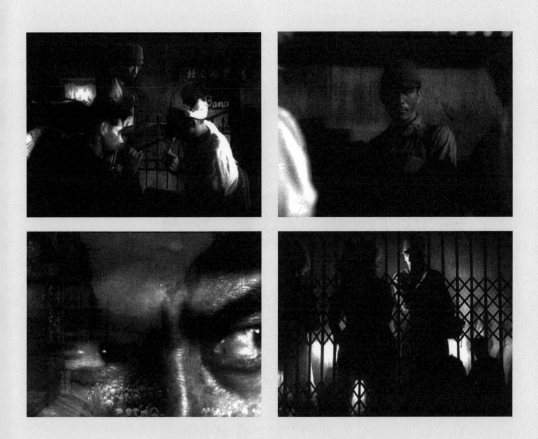

# TOKYO STORY (1953)

*Ginza shopping district*

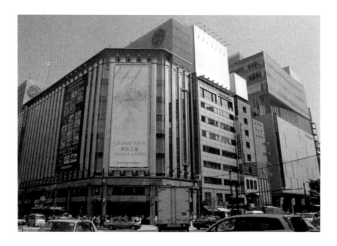

**IN THIS ACKNOWLEDGED** masterpiece of film history, Yasujiro Ozu puts his muse actress Setsuko Hara in the role of angel and guide. An elderly couple living in western Japan comes to Tokyo, to visit their children and grandchildren, all of whom have little time to spare them. Schemes fail to entertain the parents, and it will be up to Noriko, the widow of their youngest son, fallen in the war, to show them the heart of Tokyo. The pulse of the city beats strongest in Ginza in the daytime, with office workers, shoppers and visitors making their way between the Imperial Palace in the Chiyoda area to the famous department stores which mark Ginza's large avenues. Noriko takes them on a guided bus tour, stopping to climb the stairs of one such store offering a panoramic view of the city. Her in-laws inquire as to the geography of their children's home as Tokyo sprawls before them. Setsuko Hara is the compass to the soul of the city. The sequence closes with her bringing the old couple back to her own modest one-room flat, where she lives alone. With no kitchen to speak of, she discreetly orders food and borrows sake from her neighbour. The journey proves too much for the mother, and the kindness shown by Noriko seals a tacit pact between her and her father-in-law. Such are the bonds that make up the foundations of Ozu's cinema. •➤*Stephen Sarrazin*

**Above** Mitsukoshi Ginza (Photo ©Tom Baker)

*Directed by Yasujiro Ozu*
**Scene description:** *Ginza sightseeing*
**Timecode for scene:** *0:37:26 – 0:38:30*

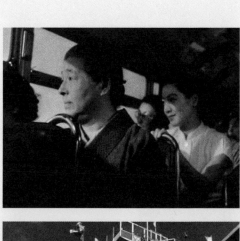
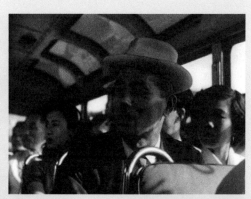
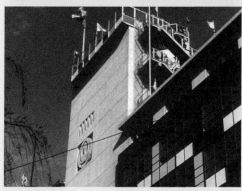
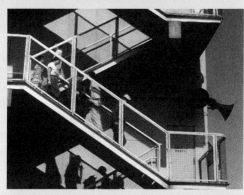
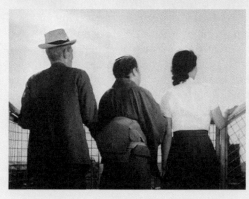
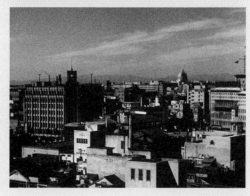

# WHERE CHIMNEYS ARE SEEN (1953)

LOCATION *Senju Thermal Power Station, 35 Senju Sakuragi, Adachi Ward*

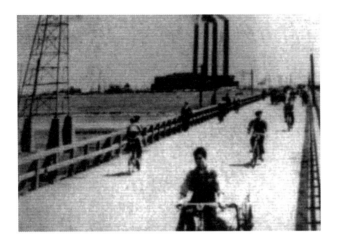

**THE FOUR *OBAKE-ENTOTSU*** ('monster chimneys') of the Senju Thermal Power Station were a beloved landmark of downtown Tokyo between 1925 and 1964. The urban legend of these chimneys that stood on the banks of the Sumida River in Adachi-ku was that depending on where you saw them there could appear to be four, three, two, or even one chimney. Director Heinosuke Gosho featured the Senju chimneys as a powerful all-seeing presence in his nuanced 1953 *shomin-geki*, or 'common people's drama', *Where Chimneys Are Seen*. Hiroko (Kinuyo Tanaka), a war widow now remarried to a store clerk, lives in a downtown tenement where many believe there are only three chimneys. One day, a co-worker tells Hiroko that a ragged man carrying a baby was asking around for her address. Puzzled, she walks home and, looking up, she sees only two chimneys. Still traumatized from the war Hiroko dashes up the riverbank and is relieved to see the usual three chimneys are there, but there is still doubt on her face. Arriving home she finds the baby left in her bedroom. Hiroko's neighbors all become involved in solving the mystery of who this child is, but perhaps the baby was sent from the monster chimneys themselves. The ageing Senju Thermal Power Station was demolished in 1964, and now a raw materials depot has replaced the iconic chimneys, but visitors to the Senju campus of Teikyo Science University can still see a portion of one of the *obake-entotsu* preserved in a special monument. **⊷Reiko Tahara**

**Above** An early photograph of the 'obake-entosu' (Photo ©tinyurl.com/6h48qoc)

*Directed by Heinosuke Gosho*
*Scene description: Hiroko runs to see the monster chimneys*
*Timecode for scene: 0:33:56 – 0:34:09*

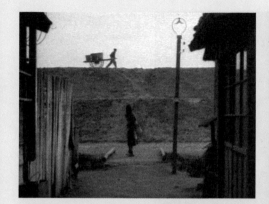 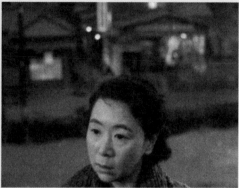

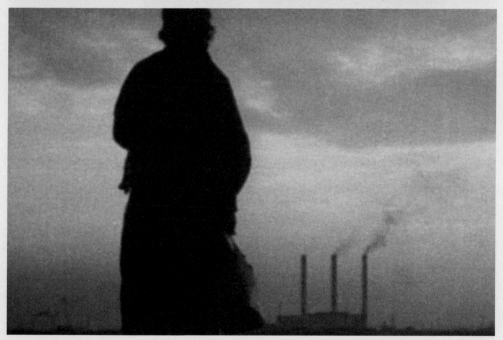

# GODZILLA/GORIJA (1954)

*Wako Department Store, 4-5-11 Ginza, Chūō*

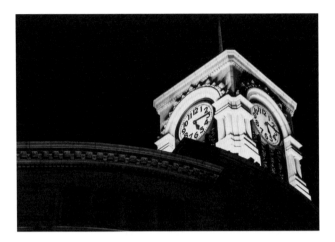

**DURING THE STRATEGIC BOMBINGS** of World War II, most of the Ginza – Tokyo's most upscale shopping district – was destroyed, but one building that avoided being reduced to rubble was the Wako Department Store, a neo-Renaissance structure designed by Jin Watanabe. Although the real-life building survived allied air raids, its miniature equivalent in Ishirō Honda's *kaijū eiga* classic *Godzilla* would not have such good fortune. After arriving in Tokyo and breaking through a military-constructed electric fence, Godzilla hits the Ginza in one of the most destructive displays of cinematic tourism ever committed to celluloid, setting fire to the surrounding buildings with his atomic breath while bystanders run for cover. The gonging clock at the top of the Wako building irritates Godzilla just as much as the military planes and tanks that have been sent to end his rampage, so the titular monster tears down the tower; however, the various human reactions to crisis are as significant as the spectacle. A terrified mother consoles her children by telling them, 'You can see your father soon, we'll join him in heaven', while the excitable newsman on the scene provides a report – 'Incredible! Unbelievable! But it's a fact! It's happening before our eyes. There's a sea of fire behind Godzilla… What you see is not a movie, it's utterly bizarre, as though history has been turned back two million years' – that suggests he is in awe of the monster. Satisfied by his 'shopping spree', Godzilla then stomps away from the Ginza, heading to Hibiya. **John Berra**

(Photo ©tinyurl.com/69o5otx)

*Directed by Ishirō Honda*
**Scene description: Godzilla hits the Ginza**
**Timecode for scene: 0:57:58 - 1:00:42**

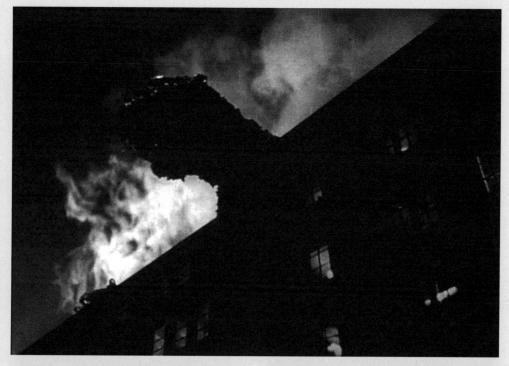

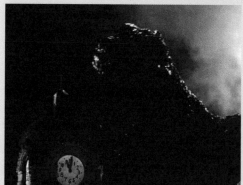 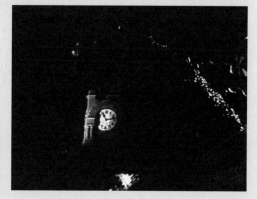

# HOUSE OF BAMBOO (1955)

LOCATION *Ginza district of Chūō*

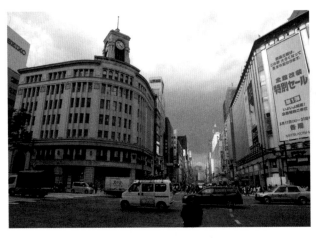
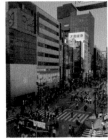

**HOUSE OF BAMBOO WAS THE FIRST** US production to film in Japan, and thanks to the cooperation of the US military and the Japanese and Tokyo government, it was granted access to some spectacular locations, including the Ginza, which becomes a key location during a foiled heist. The now popular shopping destination was designated as an area of modernization by the Meiji government during the 1870s. When it came time to film *House of Bamboo*, Ginza had been rebuilt after being levelled during the Allied fire-bombings. This gave Fuller the image of modernity he was looking for, as the buildings were not only new, but many were also western in their design. Sandy (Robert Ryan) and his gang are attempting an armoured car heist in Ginza; however, they quickly call it off when they discover someone in their ranks has tipped off the cops. Like most of the film, Fuller sets up each key scene with expansive CinemaScope shots, in this case a busy Ginza intersection surrounded by massive modern buildings, to help establish the tone of Japan he envisions – a romantic collision of the ancient and the modern, tradition with technology. These establishing shots were taken on location, but all close-ups were produced on sound stages, cutting away to an idyllic and fictitious Ginza where geisha walk the streets. Fuller presents a heightened post-war vision of Tokyo to give the American audiences something familiar and yet something exotic, humanizing the once reviled war-time enemy. **➻ Matthew Hardstaff**

(Photos ©Yu Masui / ©Emily Red)

*Directed by Samuel Fuller*
**Scene description: The failed armoured car heist**
**Timecode for scene: 1:15:45–1:19:15**

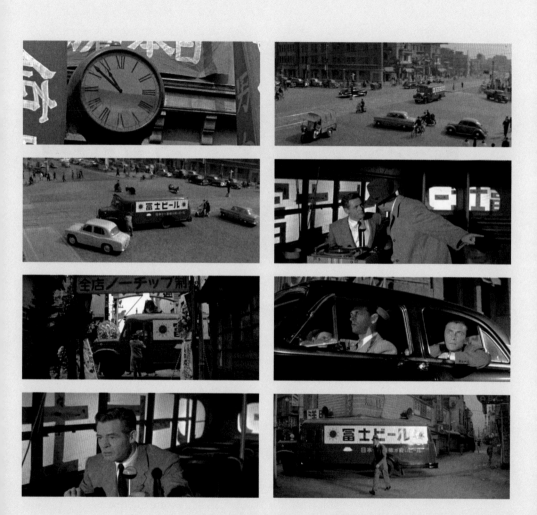

# WHEN A WOMAN ASCENDS THE STAIRS (1960)

LOCATION *Ginza 6-chome*

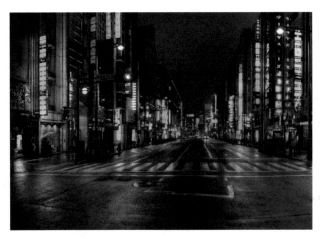
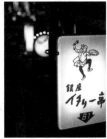

**IN MIKIO NARUSE'S** depiction of Ginza's new floating world, and its blossoming of hostess bars, iconic actress Hideko Takamine acts as both guide and protagonist. Once again she plays the woman facing an unwelcomed fate, the loss of her husband, with dignity. In the world of westernized young women enticing businessmen to drink, Takamine's demure grace, her seemingly unattainable desires and her intelligence, make her irresistible to all generations of Japanese men, from the business leader played by frequent Takamine partner, Masayuki Mori, to sixties' young lion Tatsuya Nakadai's bar manager. Naruse relies on the actress' voice-over, in a knowing tone, to explain how Ginza expanded and how women came to acquire small bars and become business owners. How one generation, on the wane, hopes to find a husband while the other sees no purpose in it. Through Takamine's character, Keiko Yashiro (aka Mama), the film reveals the uncompromising world of debts, and how inexperienced 'entrepreneurs' have nowhere to hide. Naruse accomplishes this in recurrent shots of Mama making her way through the narrow Ginza streets, a procession of encountered clients entering and exiting the hundreds of bars lining her path, until she reaches the stairs that lead up to where she faces the choice of becoming a fading queen or go into business for herself. But Mama is far too wise and knows her way better than any along the Ginza night streets. **•❖Stephen Sarrazin**

**Above** Ginza street and neon restaurant sign (Photos ©www.tokyoform.com / ©cocoip)

*Directed by Mikio Naruse*
**Scene description: Hostess life**
*Timecode for scene: 0:16:10 – 0:16:48*

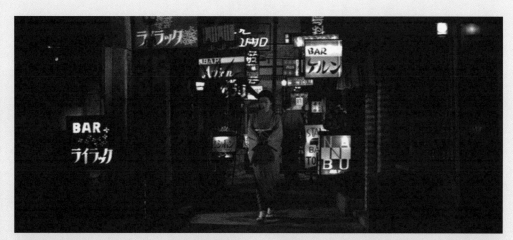

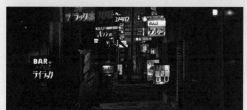
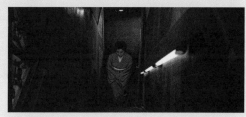

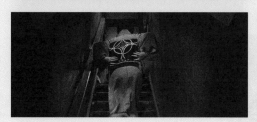
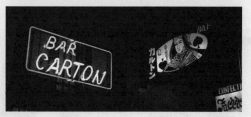

# WORST OF TIMES / BEST OF TIMES

## Post-War Tokyo in Film

Text by
ERIC EVANS

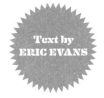

**NEAR THE END OF HIS FILM** *Kabei: Our Mother* (2008), Yoji Yamada shocks us. In the span of 30 seconds, he elegantly communicates the horrible effect that allied bombings of World War II had on Tokyo without noise or voice. One moment the mother of the title, Kayo Nogami (Sayuri Yoshinaga), is gazing down her alleyway to the main street, sakura trees blooming as neighbours pass by the shops. Standing at the same vantage point a few moments later, her gaze reaches a far horizon as the city has been razed to the ground, the ruins dotted with charred tree stumps.

Yamada is a master sentimentalist whose skills have been sharpened by decades of popular film-making. The *Tora-san* series, for which he wrote all 48 screenplays and directed all but two installments, is built upon nostalgia, unrequited love and heartbreak. As a result of this facility with the tugging of heartstrings, Yamada has artfully elevated enjoyable but essentially unremarkable fare like *Twilight Samurai* and *The Hidden Blade* to contemporary classic status. But in *Kabei* it is not the drafting and wartime death of a sensitive main character that conveys the shock of the war, but rather that simple, stark visual. Why would that be? Surely the destruction of large sections of Tokyo during the war had been documented in other Japanese films, hadn't it?

The post-war period (1945–60) was a particularly vital time for Japanese film. During that span directors such as Akira Kurosawa, Kenji Mizoguchi, and Yasujiro Ozu all received international attention for their work, and the Academy Awards additionally recognized and/or awarded *Jigoku* (Teinosuke Kinugasa), *Samurai: The Legend of Musashi* (Hiroshi Inagaki), and *The Burmese Harp* (Kon Ichikawa) in the category of Best Foreign Film. Tellingly, only two of these seven films are set in contemporary times, and while Ichikawa's film deals with the agonies of war, neither focuses on the devastation visited upon the Japanese capital. A travelogue of sorts, *Tokyo Story* (Yasujiro Ozu, 1953) offers up several opportunities to show, if not at least comment on, the rebuilding necessary after the war. Yet Ozu opts to sidestep the issue, as in the scene in which Shukichi and Tomi Hiyayama (Chishu Ryu and Chieko Higashiyama), spurned by their own children, are shown the city by their widowed

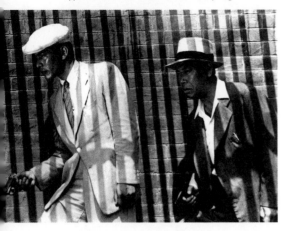

daughter-in-law (Setsuko Hara).

Ozu frames the shot from halfway down a stairwell behind the actors, so that we cannot see what the Hiyayamas see. It's a curious choice not to share that view, even in the form of a cutaway in the event the location itself was on a set. No one spends sightseeing time focusing on rebuilding efforts, but during sequences in which the trio tour the city in a bus and look out over vast expanses, nothing is seen which even hints at the massive destruction just a few years past. Having never visited the city, the Hiyayamas speak of their astonishment at the sheer size of Tokyo, something easier shown than described. Later, as they look over a different (yet similarly hidden) view of the city, they remark 'if we got lost, we'd never find each other again'.

Ozu's practical, down-to-earth style more or less demands a simple visual of the city skyline to underscore his characters' sense of wonder and astonishment, yet none follows. We can see a hint at the city's wonders in the form of a single building just right of Tomi, but nothing that suggests scope. In fairness, by the time filming started in July 1953 much of the wartime devastation had been replaced by a newer, more modern Tokyo, but newspaper reports from the mid-1940s estimate that in certain parts of the city – Asakusa, for

> **The sight of a city in flames, was brought painfully to life by the atomic breath of Godzilla the destroyer, a monster representing the atomic bomb.**

instance – a full 50 per cent of the buildings had been demolished. Any expansive view of Tokyo would include gaps made even more pronounced by the appearance of modern, multi-story buildings. Ozu's seeming refusal to allow the audience to share his characters' gaze is puzzling.

Ozu isn't alone. Many films of the 1940s and 1950s, including those filmed in the capital just after the war, similarly avoid footage of the city. Even a gritty noir like *Nora Inu/Stray Dog* (Akira Kurosawa) hints at, more than shows, the devastation. It might be a blithe view, but films such as *Stray Dog* and *Record of a Tenement Gentleman* (Yasujiro Ozu) might have benefited from the legitimacy showing the more damaged parts of the city would have allowed. This may confuse us now, but this absence of destruction on-screen was a direct result of the sanitary censorship policies of the US Occupying Forces.

Of course the destruction of Tokyo has been shown on film, and to great effect, in the Japanese cinema of the 1950s. But it wasn't the Allied bombings that toppled buildings and set entire neighborhoods alight, but a metaphorical manifestation of the horrible weapons that ended the war. The sight of a city in flames, still fresh in the minds of millions of survivors of the hostilities not a decade old, was brought painfully to life by the atomic breath of Godzilla the destroyer, a monster representing the atomic bomb. *Gorija/Godzilla* (Ishirō Honda, 1954) is a terrifying example of man's self-destructive hubris. Nuclear detonations bring destruction to the city in a natural form, but the message was painfully clear: we did this to ourselves.

*Kabei* doesn't need to show planes swooping out of the sky or bombs dropping to convey the terrible aftermath of World War II. Yamada wordlessly communicates those things by giving us what Ozu couldn't: a simple view of the city. In seeing what his character sees, the viewer knows a sense of loss commensurate with the destruction of everything you know, beginning with the neighborhood around you. By the time Kabei learns of a much more personal loss, that of a fallen friend, she is resolute. Her life has changed as Tokyo has changed, and all that's left for her to do is rebuild. ✤

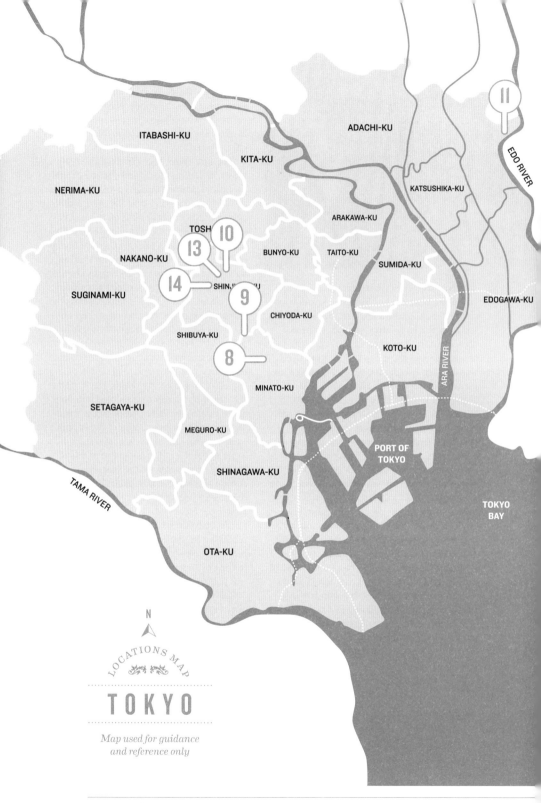

ITABASHI-KU

KITA-KU

ADACHI-KU

EDO RIVER

NERIMA-KU

KATSUSHIKA-KU

ARAKAWA-KU

TOSH

10

13

NAKANO-KU

BUNYO-KU

TAITO-KU

SUMIDA-KU

EDOGAWA-KU

14

SHINJU...KU

SUGINAMI-KU

9

CHIYODA-KU

ARA RIVER

SHIBUYA-KU

KOTO-KU

8

MINATO-KU

SETAGAYA-KU

MEGURO-KU

PORT OF
TOKYO

SHINAGAWA-KU

TOKYO
BAY

TAMA RIVER

OTA-KU

N

LOCATIONS MAP

TOKYO

*Map used for guidance
and reference only*

# TOKYO LOCATIONS

## SCENES 8-14

# TOKYO OLYMPIAD (1965)

LOCATION *Japan National Route 20 between Nihonbashi and Fuchu*

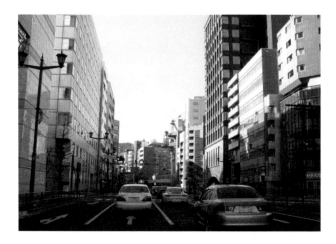

**KON ICHIKAWA'S** documentary of the 1964 Tokyo Olympics famously incited controversy upon its release, in part because it does little to show off the city itself. The exception to this is the long marathon sequence, which Ichikawa saw as the climactic moment of the Summer Games. It opens with a soaring helicopter view of the newly-built National Olympic Stadium in Kasumigaoka and showcases miles of impeccable city streets lined with enthusiastic spectators, serious officials, and a modern city which had in less than two decades remarkably risen from the ashes of World War II. The route followed part of the ancient Kōshū Kaidō – one of the Five Edo Routes. It historically began at Nihonbashi and connected Edo via 44 stations to Shimosuwa in what is now known as Nagano Prefecture. Today, the National Route 20 follows parts of the Kōshū Kaidō from Nihonbashi through Shinjuku and out of Tokyo in a westerly direction. The marathon followed this route until the turning point in Fuchū, before heading back to the stadium. Ichikawa captures the drama of this spectacular event with Abebe Bikila, showing no signs of his recent bout with appendicitis, taking a commanding early lead to become the first two-time Olympic marathon champion. At the Fuchū turning point, Jim Hogan is hot on Bikila's heels but then dramatically drops out of the race after 22 miles due to dehydration. Kōkichi Tsuburaya heartbreakingly loses out on the silver to Basil Heatley in the final sprint to the finish line. **••Catherine Munroe Hotes**

(Photo ©Aimaimyi)

*Directed by Kon Ichikawa*
**Scene description: The marathon**
**Timecode for scene: 2:16:31 – 2:24:48**

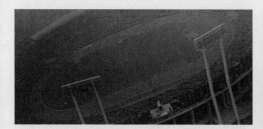 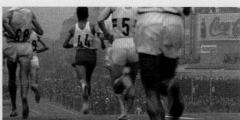

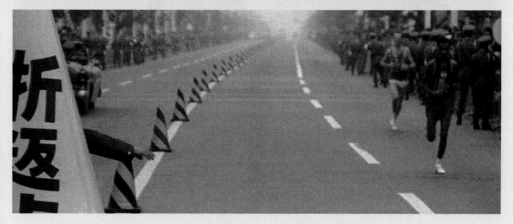

# YOU ONLY LIVE TWICE (1967)

*New Otani Hotel, 4-1 Kioicho, Chiyoda*

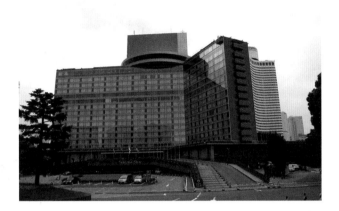

**TOKYO'S 1964** Summer Olympics showcased post-war Japan's re-emergence, announcing their status as an economic power and technological leader. The world looked on with fascination, both at the 'exoticism' of traditional Japan and the modernity and technical innovation of the new. It was the natural setting for the 1967 James Bond film, *You Only Live Twice*. Locations extended from Tokyo to the volcanoes of Kagoshima. One particularly memorable location was Chiyoda-ku's New Otani Hotel, built to coincide with the Olympics. The hotel and its rooftop revolving restaurant stand in for the headquarters of Osato Chemicals – a front for the evil organization SPECTRE. Many scenes, including car chases, gun-battles and roof-top helicopter landings, take place around the actual site. However, it is the sleek, Ken Adam-designed interior that is best remembered: the setting for furious hand-to-hand and sword combat with a hulking henchman and, later, a meeting with a sultry redhead who, with the aid of stereotypical Japanese minions and 1967-style high tech, uncover Bond's identity. The set, with its sleek mid-century modern industrial design and classical Japanese elements is a perfect reflection of the 'new' Japan of the mid-1960s. Though two additional towers have been added nearby, the New Otani of YOLT remains well-maintained and virtually unchanged, including the surrounding sixteenth century gardens. Located a short walk from Akasakamitsuke station on the Marunouchi line, it is definitely worth visiting. Recommended are vodka-martinis in the rooftop restaurant that played Osato's office. Few views of Tokyo are as beautiful or serene. **→ James Heron**

(Photo ©Ryoku Kasinn)

*Directed by Lewis Gilbert*
**Scene description: Osato and Helga see through Bond's cover**
**Timecode for scene: 0:37:01 – 0:39:08**

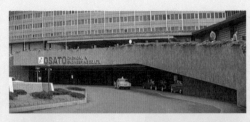 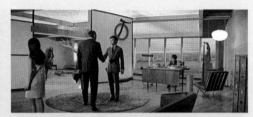

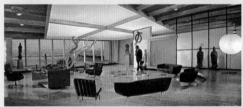 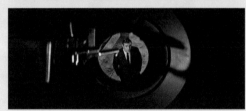

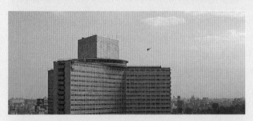 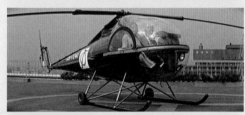

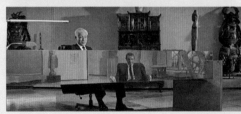 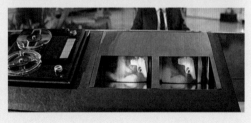

# DIARY OF A SHINJUKU THIEF (1969)

LOCATION *Kinokuniya Bookstore, 3-17-7 Shinjuku, Shinjuku-ku*

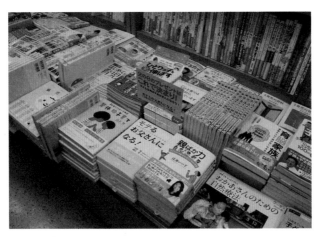
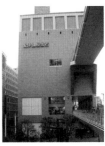

**DIARY OF A SHINJUKU THIEF** is one the most experimental works of Nagisa Oshima, a very free adaptation of Jean Genet's novel *The Thief's Journal*. The film is, among other things, a peek into a period of social, political and artistic unrest that swept Japan in 1969. We can almost feel the tumultuous atmosphere of the time. Oshima and his team gift us with obscure but powerful images of avant-garde theater, youth protest and sexual revolution, but perhaps the real protagonist of the film is Shinjuku, with the crowded street, the people, the places, and its electric atmosphere. Shinjuku's main Kinokuniya Bookstore, founded in 1927, is the locus for film. Originally the company dealt in wood and charcoal, but after Tokyo was demolished by the Great Kanto Earthquake its president Moichi Tanabe shifted his focus to pulp and paper in the form of books. In the first scene, shot guerrilla-style in the store, we are introduced to the main character, Torio Okanoue (the famous artist Tadanori Yokoo). Okanoue wanders among the shelves in the midst of a chaotic crowd shopping for or just leafing through books. Often, the people in the shop look directly at the camera, while the eye of the camera erratically follows Okanoue leaving him, diving into the stream of humanity, and finally rejoining him when he steals a couple of books. Okanoue later faces up to his crime by being escorted into the office of the real-life Moichi Tanabe who makes a cameo appearance. •❖*Matteo Boscarol*

(Photo ©tinyurl.com/66robym)

*Directed by Nagisa Oshima*
**Scene description: Shoplifting in Kinokuniya**
**Timecode for scene: 0:04:26 – 0:06:05**

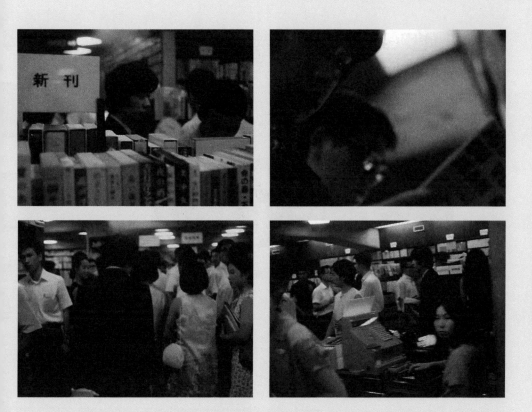

# TORA SAN: IT'S TOUGH BEING A MAN (1969)

LOCATION *Shibamata Taishakuten Sando, 7-3-12 Shibamata, Katsusika-ku*

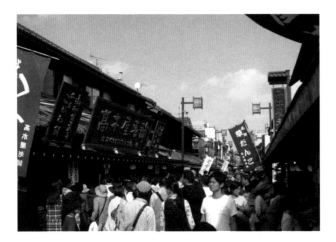

**AFTER 48 FILMS SPANNING** 36 years, the name Tora-san is indelibly linked to the character's hometown of Shibamata. The beloved tramp may have been a vagabond travelling all over Japan, but he always came back to visit (and vex) his family in the Katsushima ward town where they ran a small sweets and refreshment shop. Tora-san's importance to the area is clear as you step off the Kanamachi line at Shibamata station to be greeted by a life-size statue of actor Kiyoshi Atsumi in character, the suitcase that held all his belongings in hand. However, Tora-san is not Shibamata's only claim to fame. Minutes from the station, the Shoutengai shopping district is known for its many traditional Japanese sweet shops and *unagi* restaurants. Walk up the Shoutengai starting at around the intersection of Shibamata-kaido and Taishakuten-sando – these storefronts have remained more or less unchanged for the last century. Continue towards the temple and marvel at what looks and feels like the Tokyo of yesteryear. For more about the films, a short walk east will yield the Tora-san Museum inside the Katsushika-ku Culture Center. *It's Tough Being a Man*, the first film in the series, features Tora's first day back since running away from home as a teen. He finds a small festival in progress and, as is his style, insinuates himself into the proceedings. The narrow Shoutengai, lined with shops and teeming with revellers, looks the same today as it does on-screen despite having been filmed over four decades ago.
**↝ Eric Evans**

(Photo ©Aimaimyi, GEOlocation.ws)

*Directed by Yoji Yamada*
**Scene description: Homecoming (re)introduction to Shibamata**
*Timecode for scene: 0:03:12 – 0:05:37*

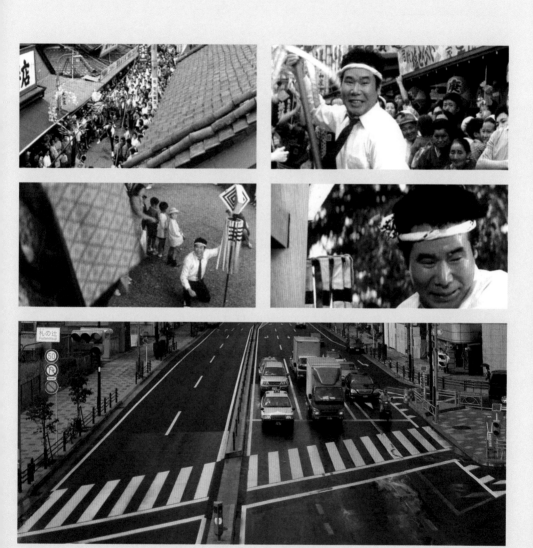

Images ©1969 Shôchiku Eiga

# IF YOU WERE YOUNG: RAGE (1970)

LOCATION   *Various locations in Tokyo*

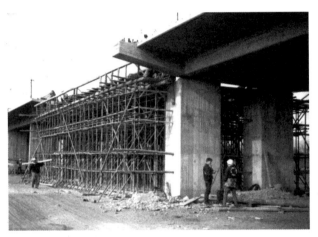
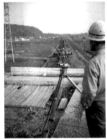

**THE SETTING OF KINJI** Fukasaku's *If You Were Young: Rage* is significant not so much for where it takes place, but when. It shows Tokyo at the tail end of its post-war reconstruction, when the spurt to rebuild the city and return the country to the fold of civilized nations (a development that peaked with the Tokyo Olympics in 1964) was winding down and many of those who had come from all over the country to make their living as construction workers found themselves out of a job. The two young heroes of the film, Asao (Gin Maeda) and Kikuo (Tetsuo Ishidate) are examples of this generation, who were gloriously dubbed the 'Golden Eggs'. When we meet them, they have been reduced to little more than cracked shells. They nevertheless fight back by choosing a life as freelancer contractors instead, as they collectively buy a dump truck which they evocatively christen 'Independence No. 1'. Many of Fukasaku's heroes are free souls whose roaring energy is eventually hemmed in by the increasingly corporate, rule-bound society of modern Japan. The young men in *If You Were Young: Rage* similarly find their dream squashed by corporate culture and the human instinct to conform, as the country closes the post-war chapter for good and gears up for its new role as a worldwide economic superpower – a position in which there no longer is any room for independence. **•• Tom Mes**

**Above** Building the Tokyo of the future in 1962 (Photo ©tinyurl.com/69qrx3n)

*Directed by Kinji Fukasaku*
**Scene description: Youth gone to waste**
**Timecode for scene: 0:29:58 – 0:31:17**

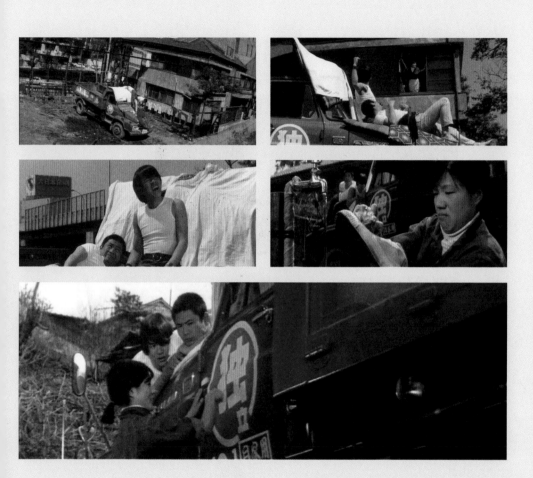

# THROW AWAY YOUR BOOKS AND RALLY IN THE STREETS (1971)

*Shinjuku Streets*

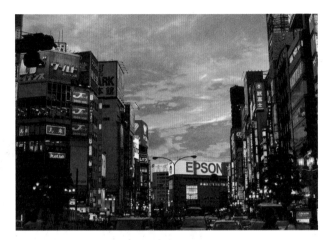

**ENRAGED BY THE** Anti-Subversive Law (1952), the ANPO Treaty (US-Japan Security Treaty), the Vietnam War and the US control of Okinawa, the angry youth of Tokyo took to the streets of Shinjuku between the 1950s and 1970s. These youths were divided into two groups: one believed in revolution and firebombs; the other in peace and acoustic guitars. Shinjuku accommodated both. On International Anti-War Day in 1968, 2,000 youths took over Shinjuku Station and blocked trains to stop fuel transportation to the US military base – 450 were arrested. In 1969, 7,000 'folk guerrillas' met in Shinjuku's underground pathways and sang anti-war songs – 64 were arrested. Still the Vietnam War continued, the ANPO was renewed twice, and their parents were busy with Japan's rapid economic growth. Shuji Terayama, a charismatic theatre director/poet, crystallizes the post-ANPO generation's disenchantment, anger and complex hatred and nostalgia for their absent parents and their lost nation in this eccentric 1971 feature film. This scene opens with a girl talking to police officers in a busy intersection in Shinjuku. A chubby boy nearby holds a giant phallic object. 'It's just a sandbag with Buddhist sutra written on it for people to punch away their frustrations,' she explains. They run away. A young man smashes books on the street and the angry youth quickly take over. A psychedelic rock number carries the lyrics of 'Wars – for whom? Peace – for whom? Masturbations – for whom? Getting arrested – your fault!' ➼*Reiko Tahara*

(Photo ©Joi Ito)

*Directed by Shuji Terayama*
**Scene description: The 1970s Youth Revolt in Shinjuku**
**Timecode for scene: 0:20:12 – 0:22:06**

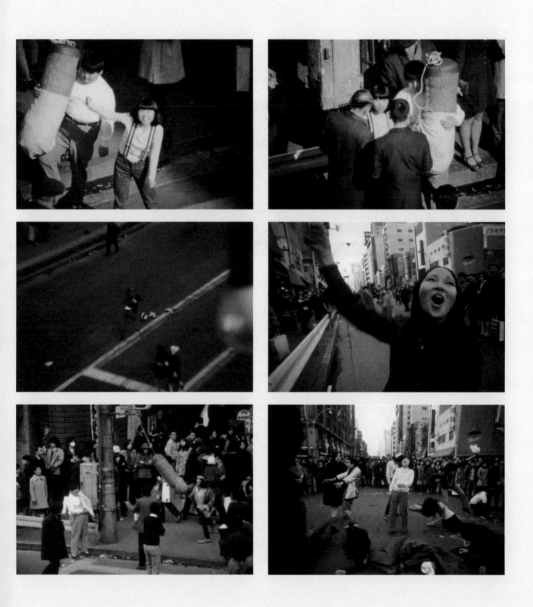

Images ©1971 Art Theatre Guild

# THE YAKUZA (1972)

*Shinjuku Tokyu Milano Building*

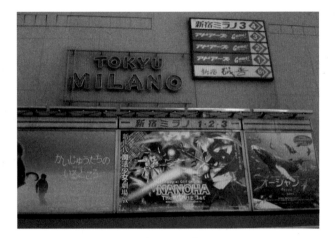

**IN THE YAKUZA**, Robert Mitchum plays the world-weary Harry Kilmer, who returns to Japan to help a friend involved in bad business with a yakuza clan. Years earlier, he had fallen in love with a Japanese woman named Eiko (Keiko Kishi) and tried to marry her, only to return to the United States alone. Once back in the East, he is reunited with Eiko as well as her brother Ken (Ken Takakura), a former yakuza who uses his familiarity with the criminal underworld to assist Harry. At one point in the film, Ken ventures into the Kabukicho. Crossing a noisy square as rain falls, he enters a pachinko parlor and meets with a contact. The real yakuza have been known to operate in the area, making its appearance in Sydney Pollack's film all too fitting – though a more likely reason for the location choice is the photogenic appeal of the many storefronts, advertisements and movie posters on display. The once-plentiful selection of Kabukicho's old movie theatres have thinned in recent years due to redevelopment and the expanding popularity of digital cinemas, though the Shinjuku Tokyu Milano Building seen in the film is still in service as of this writing. The pachinko parlor Ken visits is also still running, currently under the name Oriental Passage Pachinko and Slot.
➻*Marc Saint-Cyr*

(Photo ©Kesenaitsumi)

*Directed by Sidney Pollack*
*Scene description: Business in Kabukicho*
*Timecode for scene: 1:01:59 – 1:03:01*

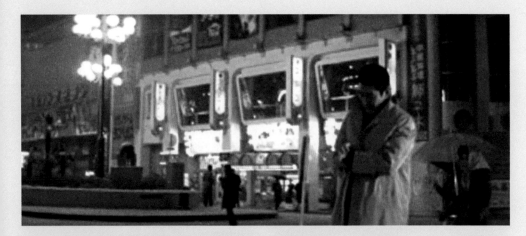

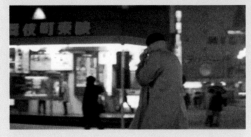 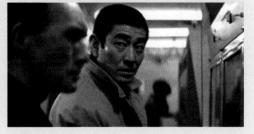

Images ©1974 Warner Bros. Pictures; Toei Company

# TOKYO MUST BURN!

*Text by*
**SAMUEL JAMIER**

## *The end of the world through anime eyes*

'Well, I still love Tokyo... even as it is now. Where else on earth do so many people enjoy their descent into destruction?' – **TOKYO BABYLON**

**JAPAN SHARES WITH AMERICA** the fantasy of its own destruction. One way or another, Tokyo must go... preferably in an apocalyptic blaze of glory. One anime after another, with implacable regularity, the megacity, which stands as a metonymy for the entire archipelago and its civilization, must be wiped off the map.

The omnipresent fascination for end-of-days cataclysms in the world of anime is closely linked to the physical existence of Japan. By nature, the archipelago is both a precarious and post-apocalyptic entity. It has long withstood earthquakes, tsunamis and typhoons on a massive scale.

Tokyo itself sits at the meeting site of three tectonic plates and is sometimes described as 'the city waiting to die'. No wonder anime narratives show the megalopolis as the perfect magnet for natural disasters and present its future in an array of 'no-future' scenarios.

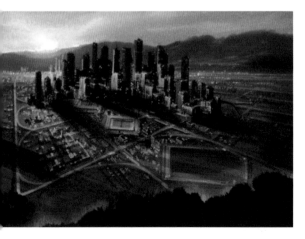

As a mode of representation, anime provides a fit surface for these dark fantasies, from *Akira* to *Tokyo Magnitude 8.0* (Masaki Tachibana and Natsuko Takahashi, 2009). While dealing directly with the anguish of (impending) annihilation, whether in serial or feature film form, the genre offers the soft comfort of its two-dimensionality or 'superflatness', to abuse Takashi Murakami's expression, contentedly operating outside the norms of realism.

Central to the apocalyptic imagination in anime are of course 'Little Boy', the atomic bomb that was dropped on Hiroshima on 6 August 1945, and 'Fat Man', Nagasaki, 9 August. Although Tokyo was spared this fate, it was subject to intense bombing during World War II. On 9 and 10 March 1945, allied bombers dropped 1,700 tons of incendiary bombs on the capital, destroying 16 square miles of the city and killing about 100,000 people – more than the total number of direct casualties in Hiroshima or Nagasaki.

Anime narratives address this unanswered anxiety of seeing the capital razed in the same (nuclear) fashion or blown to near oblivion again. As pointed out by Koji Okada, the creator of the *Shin Megami Tensei* series, Tokyo is often the focus of Japanese animation because it is fundamentally 'a city playing out the cycle of destruction and rebirth'.

This brings us back to the very architecture of the city. One should remember that traditional construction techniques relied primarily on wood, bamboo and paper: houses, temples, and even palaces were built that way. It was not rare for a whole neighbourhood, sometimes a city, to wind up burning to the ground. The survivors rebuilt the exact same original structures. Shintoism, with its emphasis on purity, actually embraces and echoes this never-ending cycle of life and

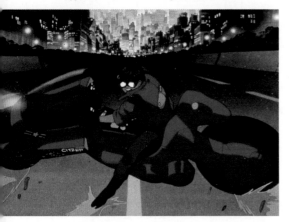

caused by demons. Based on the Great Kanto Earthquake of 1923, which destroyed much of the city, the disaster also inspired both versions of the cyberpunk epic series *Bubblegum Crisis* (1987).

Closer to actual history, the 2001 anime film *Millennium Actress*, shows Tokyo in the aftermath of World War II, and focuses on a female character who was actually born during the earthquake, a post-apocalyptic figure of sorts.

More radically, in the über-classic *Ghost in the Shell*, Tokyo has completely ceased to exist in the aftermath of a devastating war that forced the government to move to Fukuoka.

*Code Geass* (Goro Taniguchi, 2006), toys with Tokyo quite a bit by kicking off with a massacre of civilians in Shinjuku... until terrorists show up. The utter annihilation of Tokyo is around the corner.

*RahXephon* (Yutaka Izuguchi, 2007), is an interesting variation on the annihilation theme: except for Tokyo, the whole world seems to have disappeared. As it turns out, it is actually Tokyo that has been sealed off from the outside world. Nobody can enter or escape. In other words, the city is as good as dead to the world outside. When intruders manage to break through, events take a different turn, and Tokyo does not stand unscathed.

The neo-noir sci-fi TV series *Darker Than Black* (Tensai Okamura, 2007), gives the annihilation theme a name: 'The Tokyo Explosion.' As various factions try to prevent or precipitate the disaster, there is not much left of Tokyo to blow up.

A rare entry in this list, the deceptively *kawaii* series *Tokyo Magnitude 8.0* is of one the very few realistic, and therefore horrific narratives of an earthquake that turns the city to rubble. Quite unusually, the show moves towards the new territory of live cinema, convincingly appropriating its tropes.

For anime, apocalypse is then, now... and whenever. ✦

death. Shinto shrines (the Grand Shrine of Ise, for example) are typically torn down and rebuilt following the exact same design.

Apocalyptic anime is no stranger to this system. Here are a few prominent examples:

*Akira*, the 1988 anime arch-classic written and directed by Katsuhiro Otomo, blows up Tokyo *twice*. The movie sees the destruction of the city within the first few seconds of the prologue. Neo-Tokyo, built near the giant crater where the old city used to be, experiences a similar end.

It is impossible to discuss Tokyo in anime without mentioning Studio Gainax/Hideaki Anno's *Neon Genesis Evangelion* or its 2007 'update', *Rebuild of Evangelion*. The series is set in a world where Tokyo has *already* been destroyed: 'Tokyo-1' is a ruin deep underwater. Continuous assaults by giant creatures known as 'Angels' regularly wreck Tokyo-2 (built in Nagano Prefecture) and require constant rebuilding, until a final (almost nuclear) onslaught blasts city #2 to bits. Later on, the self-sacrifice of one protagonist turns a section of Tokyo-3, built on the site Hakone, into a giant crater.

**Tokyo itself sits at the meeting site of three tectonic plates and is sometimes described as 'the city waiting to die'.**

The OVA (Original Video Animation, produced for the direct-to-video market) *Demon City Shinjuku* (Yoshiaki Kawajiri, 1988), starts with the collapse of an entire chunk of Tokyo, following an earthquake

**NOTE: *This article was written on March 1, 10 days before the earthquake and tsunami hit the north coast of Japan.***

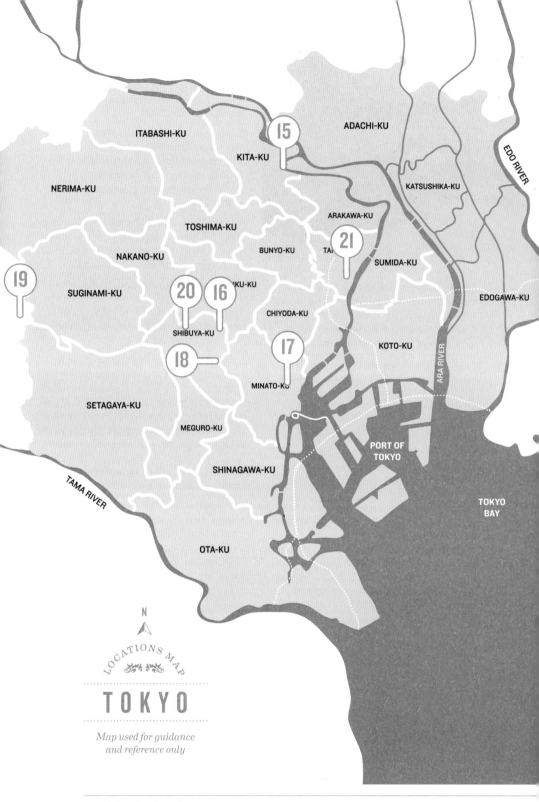

ITABASHI-KU

ADACHI-KU

KITA-KU

**15**

EDO RIVER

NERIMA-KU

KATSUSHIKA-KU

TOSHIMA-KU

ARAKAWA-KU

BUNYO-KU

TA

**21**

SUMIDA-KU

NAKANO-KU

**19**

SUGINAMI-KU

**20** **16**

KU-KU

SHIBUYA-KU

CHIYODA-KU

EDOGAWA-KU

KOTO-KU

ARA RIVER

**18**

**17**

SETAGAYA-KU

MEGURO-KU

MINATO-KU

PORT OF
TOKYO

TOKYO
BAY

SHINAGAWA-KU

TAMA RIVER

OTA-KU

N

LOCATIONS MAP

# TOKYO

*Map used for guidance
and reference only*

# TOKYO LOCATIONS

## SCENES 15-21

# NINETEEN YEAR OLD'S MAP (1979)

*Oji, Kita-ku, 1-10-18 Oji Kita*

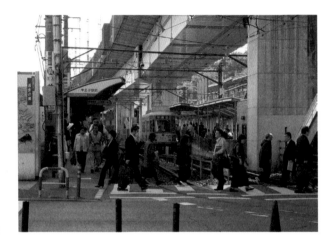

**IT IS HARD TO BELIEVE** that the slum in Yanagimachi Mitsuo's *A Nineteen Year Old's Map* was shot in Oji just a stone's throw from Ginza, the city's most expensive shopping district. Originally a suburb of Tokyo, Oji has been home to Japan's largest paper company since 1875 when a paper mill was established there. The area remained largely industrial well into the twentieth century, resulting in a slum that housed many of the mill and other factory workers. This changed drastically during the 'bubble years' when the area was rapidly gentrified when property values soared due to its proximity to Tokyo's trendiest shops. This expedient change from dwelling of the downtrodden to destination of the diamond set perfectly represents the vapid transience of Tokyo that the nameless protagonist of Yanagimachi's film deplores so much. The 19-year-old of the film's title maps out the city according to an impossible moral scale, marking any household that offends him with an X. His cynical mind is riddled with terrorist fantasies where he imagines blowing up whole neighbourhoods full of pitiful people. The film is chillingly prescient of the Aum sarin gas attacks on Tokyo which aimed to destroy the same vacuous culture that this anonymous character so deplores. In this scene, the protagonist watches a young boy receive a severe beating for stealing, but for once his hateful gaze is returned, accusing him, the idle and cold hearted moralizer, of being the real scourge of society. **•• Brandon Hocura**

**Above** Oji Station (Photo ©Tekken Sakura)

*Directed by Yanagimachi Mitsuo*
**Scene description:** *Stolen youth*
**Timecode for scene:** *0:30:39 – 0:31:15*

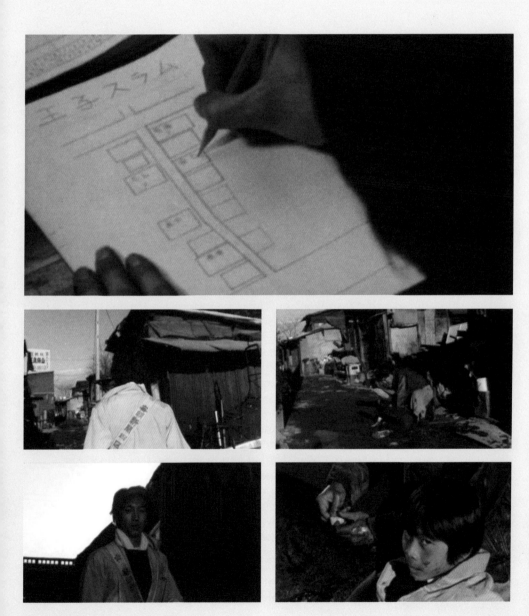

Images ©1979 Gunro

# SANS SOLEIL (1983)

LOCATION *Yoyogi Park, Kamizonocho, Yoyogi, Shibuya-ku*

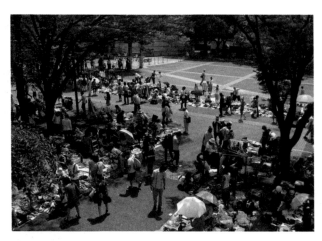
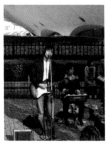

**JAPAN IS A SPECIAL PLACE** for world travelling French film-maker Chris Marker, best known for a sci-fi classic *La Jetée*. He shot three films in Japan, but *Sans Soleil* is his artistic masterpiece. Guided by the voice of an unidentified woman reading letters from fictional nomadic cameraman Sandor Krasna, it takes us to seven countries with a curious focus on Japan and Guinea-Bissau as the 'two extreme poles of survival'. He calls Japan the winner because it, as the only non-white first world nation, has achieved 'the co-existence of different concepts of time' other than Western progress. To find Japan's various modes of time, Krasna/Marker visit neighbourhood celebrations and other daily rituals - including teens dancing in Harajuku. Starting in 1977, Omotesando Street in Harajuku was closed to traffic on Sundays and holidays creating a pedestrian paradise (*hokoten*). Here, as many as 2,000 teens appeared in neon costumes and heavy make-up to dance to the disco hits of the 1980s. Known as Takenoko-zoku, or 'The Bamboo Shoot Tribe', they became Harajuku's original tourist attraction. 'They want people to look at them, but they don't seem to notice that people do. They live in a parallel time sphere,' Marker contemplates as he watches a young novice Takenoko girl learning her dance. The Harajuku Hokoten later produced the Rock 'n' Roller Tribe and numerous indie bands, but was closed in 1998 to ease traffic and to put an end to the garbage problems created by the teens. **➻Reiko Tahara**

(Photos ©Jiri Vrsecky / ©Peter Van den Bossche)

*Directed by Chris Marker*
**Scene description: Bamboo Shoot Tribe in Harajuku pedestrian paradise**
**Timecode for scene: 0:45:37 – 0:47:10**

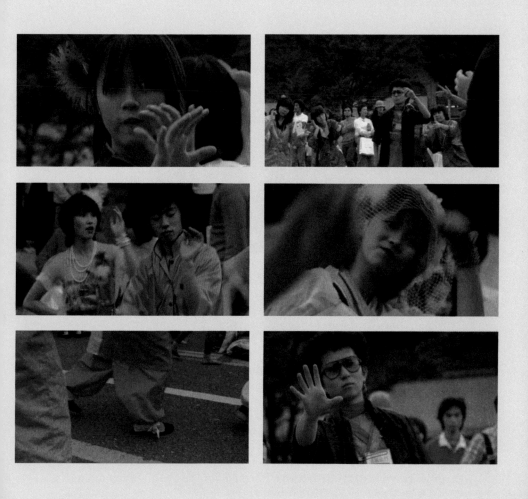

Images ©1983 Argos Films

# TOKYO-GA (1985)

LOCATION *Tokyo Tower, 4-2-8 Shibakoen Minato-ku*

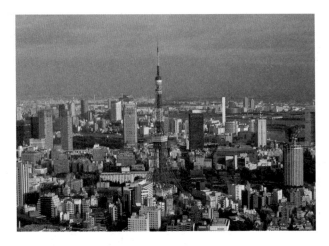

**IN 1983, WIM WENDERS** brought his camera to Tokyo in search of any remaining traces of the cinematic world of Yasujiro Ozu. In this scene, Wenders meets with friend and fellow film-maker Werner Herzog at the top of Tokyo Tower in Minato Ward. Since its completion in 1958, Tokyo Tower has captured the Japanese nation's imagination as a symbol of their capital city. Tourists flock to its observation decks to marvel at the vast expanse of metropolis below. On a clear day, one can even spot Mount Fuji to the south of the city. Herzog takes a dim view of Wenders' chances of finding anything remotely worth filming in 'this ravaged landscape' of modern Tokyo where everything is built up and there are few images that live up to Herzog's ideal of a pure, clean, and transparent image. There is an irony in Herzog's choice of words because twice during Ozu's lifetime the city of Tokyo was truly a ravaged landscape, razed to the ground by the 1923 Great Kanto Earthquake and by fire-bombings during the war. However, as Ozu's films captivatingly tell us, the heart of Tokyo is not to be found in the façades of its architecture, but in the resilient spirit of its inhabitants. Wenders instinctively realizes this and during Herzog's rant he cuts away to images of the people visiting Tokyo Tower. He fortuitously captures a father with his young children: a tender and delightful Ozu-esque moment. **••Catherine Munroe Hotes**

(Photo ©Morio)

*Directed by Wim Wenders*
*Scene description: Meeting Werner Herzog at Tokyo Tower*
*Timecode for scene: 0:52:17 – 0:53:14*

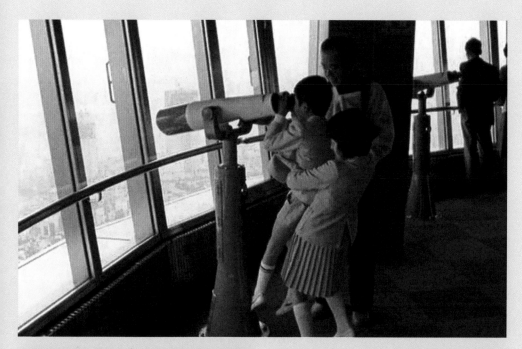

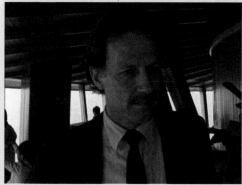
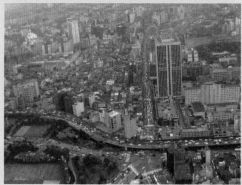

# HACHIKO MONOGATARI (1987)

LOCATION *Shibuya station, 1-1 Dogenzaka Itchōme, Shibuya*

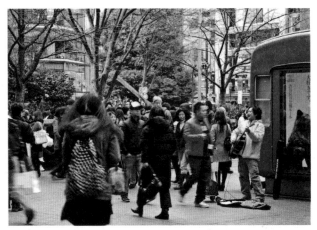 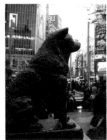

**ON THE SURFACE,** Seijiro Koyama's 1987 film *Hachiko Monogatari*, upon which 2009's *Hachi: A Dog's Tale* is based, appears to be a modest dog lovers' movie, but the film is actually based on one of the best known modern stories in Japan. Hachiko's story is truly a tale of man's best friend, a Japanese version of 'Greyfriars Bobby'. Owned by Dr Hidesaburo Ueno, a University of Tokyo professor in the late nineteenth century, Hachiko was an Akita who loyally waited for his master's return every evening at Shibuya station even ten years after the professor's death. The story of Hachiko's loyalty and filial piety became so widespread across the nation that, even before the dog's passing in 1935, a bronze statue was erected in his honor in front of Shibuya station. In this scene, probably the most tear-filled, the faithful Hachiko runs after the hearse that's carrying Dr Ueno to his final resting place. As the procession passes Shibuya station, Hachiko gives up the pursuit at approximately the exact same location that the statue currently stands. Today, Hachiko is a popular meeting spot for friends and lovers in the general hustle and bustle of modern day Shibuya as a beacon of sorts for gatherings. Perhaps that the statue is used in this manner is coincidental, but Hachiko is also a poignant reminder of those qualities we value in people: faith, loyalty and unconditional love. **Jon Jung**

**Above** Shibuya Station (Photo ©Miyuki Kobayashi) / Hachiko statue outside Shibuya station (Photo ©Alan Gratz)

*Directed by Seijiro Koyama*
**Scene description:** *The faithfulness of Hachiko*
*Timecode for scene: 1:01:41 – 1:03:29*

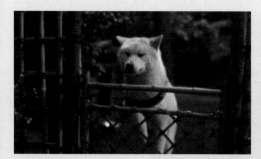 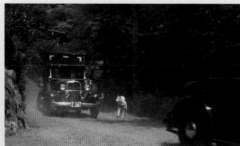

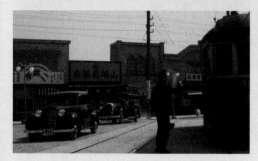 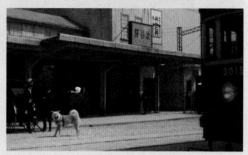

# POM POKO (1994)

*Tama New Town*

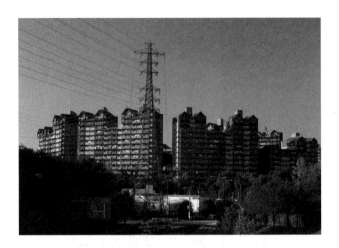

**TOKYO IS ONE OF THE** world's most crowded cities with nearly nine million people crammed into 617 square kilometres. Anyone who has called Tokyo home will be familiar with its tiny living spaces and ferociously vertical development. Skyscrapers can only be built so high though, so the annexation of the surrounding countryside became necessary to accommodate Tokyo's bursting population. Most wouldn't expect an animated film to take on the environmental ramifications of the massive suburbs that ring Tokyo, but that is exactly what anime master Isao Takahata did with his film *Pom Poko*. Set in 1967 Pom Poko shows us Tokyo's sprawl from the viewpoint of a group of *tanuki*, or raccoon dogs, who call the Tama Hills, a once forested area south west of the city, home. We first meet the *tanuki* as they're battling for a slice of their shrinking territory. The conflict is quashed by *tanuki* elder Oroku who reminds both parties who the real enemy is – the humans who are destroying their habitat with the construction of Tama New Town, a real bedroom district that now houses 300,000 displaced Tokyoites. We're filled in on the history of Japan's largest urban development project as the *tanuki* survey the devastation caused by the humans' bulldozers. 'In the past we always thought the humans were animals just like us,' admits one *tanuki* as a group of Buddha reshape the hills with their bare hands, 'but now we realized these guys were powerful... Maybe as powerful as the gods!' **→Chris MaGee**

**Above** Tama newtown, Hachioji (Photo ©Waka Moana)

*Directed by Isao Takahata*
**Scene description: The construction of New Tama**
**Timecode for scene: 0:05:17 – 0:06:37**

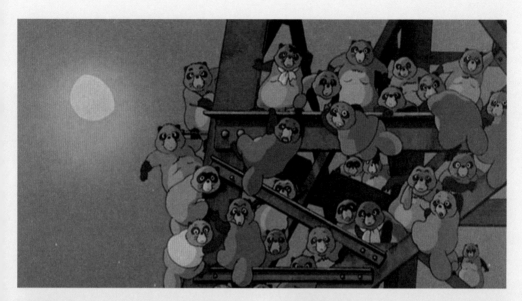

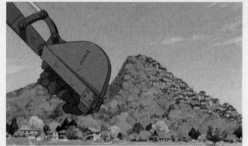

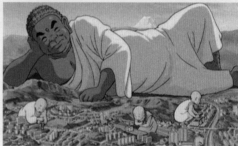

# DEAD OR ALIVE (1999)

*Kabukicho Ichibangai Gate, Kabukicho Ichibangai and Yasukuni-dori*

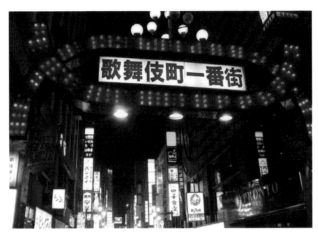
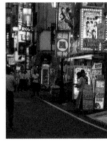

**TOKYO'S SHINJUKU WARD** is large and varied. Its attractions range from the family-friendly green haven of Shinjuku Gyoen to the anaemically corporate Skyscraper District. In films, however, and particularly in the gangster films of Takashi Miike, the image of Shinjuku boils down to the gaudy, garish, noisy pleasure quarter that is Kabukicho. Measuring little more than 600 square meters, Kabukicho is often referred to as Tokyo's red-light district, but this would be selling the area short. Hundreds of night clubs, bars, restaurants and massage parlors offer just about any form of night-time entertainment one can imagine (and quite a few one can't). It is also an area lorded over by organized crime, hence it serving as frequent background to gangster films. Foreign influence has traditionally been strong in Kabukicho: it was the Chinese that developed the area during the post-war years, after the construction of the kabuki theatre, from which the area derives its name, was abandoned. As a result, gangs of Japanese, Chinese and Korean (and lately even Nigerian) origin have long been rivals over this tiny but prosperous turf. Few films give a better impression of the hustle and bustle of Kabukicho than Takashi Miike's *Dead or Alive*, particularly its opening seven-minute montage of crime, vice and viscera. Its rapid-fire editing reflects the area's relentless all-night energy, as the camera penetrates the backstreets, the bars and the businesses, and we watch cops, thugs, strippers and hookers go about their dubious ways. ◆**Tom Mes**

(Photo ©cookieboymonster)

*Directed by Takashi Miike*
**Scene description: Welcome to Kabukicho**
**Timecode for scene: 0:00:58 – 0:04:55**

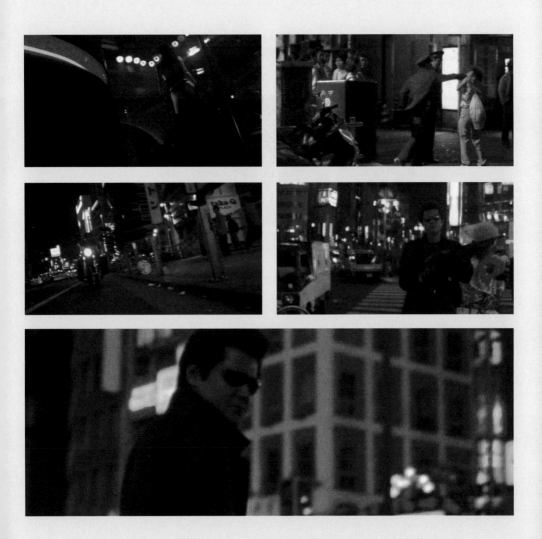

# KIKUJIRO (1999)

*Asakusa Senso-ji Temple, Nitenmon Gate*

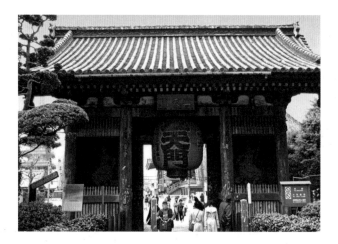

**ONE OF THE MOST FAMOUS** Tokyoites in the world has to be Takeshi 'Beat' Kitano. The 63-year-old comedian, film-maker, TV host, author and visual artist has become a one-man entertainment industry. This mindboggling fame comes in stark contrast to Kitano's childhood growing up the son of an alcoholic house painter in the impoverished neighbourhood of Umejima in Adachi-ku. At the age of 25 Kitano shuffled off his working-class roots and moved to the old entertainment district of Asakusa to pursue his dream of becoming a comedian. It was here that the Kitano the world knows today took shape. In 1999 Kitano included a cinematic love letter to Asakusa in his film *Kikujiro* which he named after his late father. It tells the story of a boy named Masao (Yusuke Sekiguchi) who spends his summer travelling to Toyohashi to search for his mother. Accompanying him on his journey is a low-level thug (Takeshi Kitano). Before Kitano even appears on-screen though he treats us to a tour of Asakusa as Masao, and his friend Yuji takes a detour to escape a group of teenage bullies. Kitano transforms the souvenir stalls selling cheap, garish trinkets around Asakusa's 1,400-year-old Senso-ji Temple into a world of colourful child-like dreams. Masao evades the bullies and eventually exits Senso-ji through the eastern Nitenmon Gate before crossing the Sakura Bridge. *Kikujiro* may end up taking its two protagonists to Aichi Prefecture, but this opening scene is a wonder-filled adventure through one of Tokyo's oldest districts. ➥*Chris MaGee*

**Above** The Nitenmon Gate of Senso-ji (Photo ©Zukk Nippon)

*Directed by Takeshi Kitano*
**Scene description: Masao and Yuji run from the bullies**
**Timecode for scene: 0:03:16 – 0:04:26**

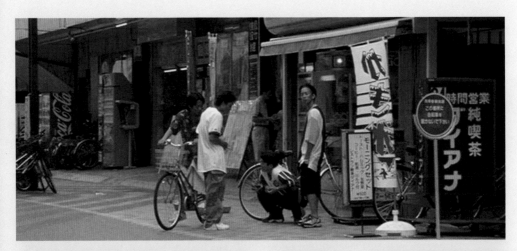

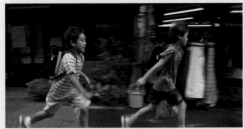

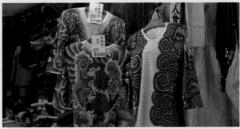

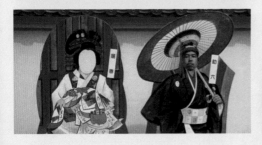

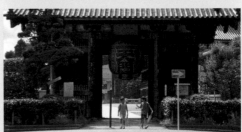

# TOKYO STORIES

Text by
JOHN
BERRA

## *The humanistic cityscape of Yasujiro Ozu*

**THROUGHOUT HIS CAREER**, Yasujiro Ozu made numerous films that were located in the Japanese capital, five of which actually had the word 'Tokyo' in the title. Such recurrence is entirely in-keeping with the nature of the director's work as actors, motifs, themes and shots would be repeated across more than 50 feature films with Ozu's output serving as a valuable record of – and commentary on – the rejuvenation, suburbanization and westernization of Tokyo. Ozu was a humanist film-maker, primarily concerned with the gradual erosion of traditional family values and the struggles of those citizens that were falling by the social-economic wayside. Therefore, the Tokyo of his oeuvre is not one of sweeping cityscapes but one of urban miniatures; his slight narratives take place in particular districts or households, while the development of Tokyo is noted in the director's trademark transition shots, such as the cutaways to automobiles, trains and telephone wires in *Tokyo Story*. Ozu was born in 1903 in the Fukagawa district of Tokyo, but at the age of ten was

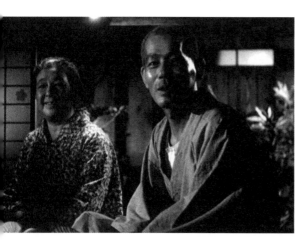

sent to his father's home town of Matsuzaka for education, then accepted a position as a teacher in a mountain village. Returning to Tokyo in 1923, Ozu entered the film industry, making his directorial debut with *The Sword of Penitence* (1927), which would be his only period piece. Ozu subsequently specialized in *shomin-geki* (films about contemporary lower- or middle-class life), with his depictions of Tokyo being informed by the social-economic circumstances of his characters.

Many accounts of Ozu's career make the convenient distinction between his pre-war and post-war periods, generally regarding his earlier output as comedic and his later works as more serious in tone. However, many of his pre-war films deal with the difficulties of surviving in Tokyo on an income that is limited or even non-existent. *Woman of Tokyo* (1933) tackles the 1930s trope of the 'modern girl' with office typist Chikako supporting the studies of her younger brother by alternating day-time corporate conformity with night-time work as cabaret hostess in the red light district; Ozu shows Chikako grooming herself for both office and nightclub, suggesting the similarities between the two professional realms and showing his heroine's need to navigate both as a means of maintaining an economic foothold. *An Inn in Tokyo* (1935) takes place in the industrial district of Koto and deals with a father-and-son forced to live hand-to-mouth due to the scarcity of work; this is a barren, depression-era Tokyo, where the characters are constantly framed against looming factories, gas containers and telegraph poles, signifiers of industry that fail to lead to regular employment. The industrial district also plays a prominent role in *The Only Son* (1936), a precursor to *Tokyo Story* in that it deals with a mother

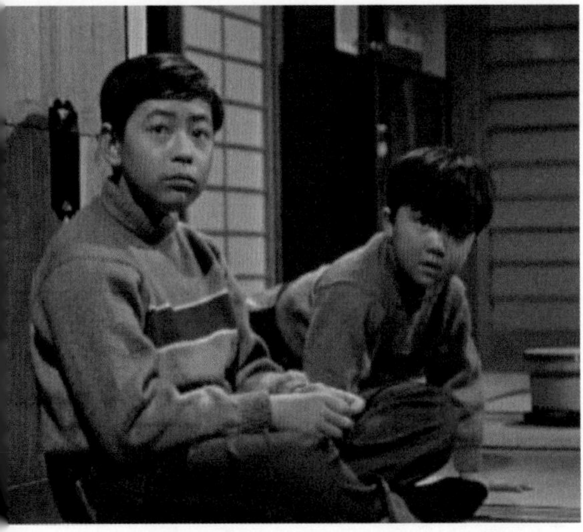

from the countryside belatedly visiting her son in Tokyo, only to have expectations of her offspring's adult life dashed by learning of his struggle to support his wife and child through a poorly-paid position as a night school teacher. The son's house is located on the edge of a wasteland where the metrical thud from the nearby factory prevents any sense of peace, while the shabby surroundings illustrate that his family is existing at the precarious edge of the social-economic spectrum.

Altogether lighter accounts of Tokyo life are offered by Ozu's splendid satires of suburbanization, *I Was Born, But...* and *Good Morning*, with the latter being a Technicolor reworking of the silent former. These suburbs are developing areas where houses seem to have sprung up on otherwise empty fields and commuter trains blast through the landscape on the fast track to modernity. Compared to the pressing economic problems of the aforementioned films, the difficulties of these suburbanites are more easily dealt with; *I Was Born, But...* revolves around the efforts of a transplanted family to adjust to the social networks of the schoolyard and the office, while the more westernized suburb of *Good Morning* is the home of two boys who try to coerce their parents into buying a television set. However, Ozu did not entirely equate suburbia with stability as evidenced by the familial tensions in *Tokyo Twilight* (1957); the home of the Sugiyama family is located in Zoshigaya, the kind of uptown residential area that should allow for a comfortable existence, but younger daughter Akiko ends up wandering around downtown Shinagawa, trying to find her boyfriend to inform him of her pregnancy and to locate her long-lost mother. Zoshigaya may be a safe area, but the eventual suicide of Akiko – who is unable to accept her mother's desertion – shows that it is not a sanctuary from familial strife, while home truths are only revealed by visiting the seedy streets, dimly-lit bars and murky mah-jong parlor of Shinagawa.

**Ozu was a humanist film-maker, primarily concerned with the gradual erosion of traditional family values and the struggles of those citizens that were falling by the social-economic wayside.**

Of course, the most revered of Ozu's masterworks remains *Tokyo Story* in which an aging couple travel from the seaside town of Onomichi to see their grown-up children in the capital. The parents explore the city by riding the public transportation system and are clearly awestruck by modern Tokyo, but are disappointed by how their children have become self-absorbed to the point that they have little time for them during their stay. As the title suggests, *Tokyo Story* is very much a summative statement by Ozu in that it pays tribute to the structural progression of the Japanese capital, while commenting on the manner in which the younger generation must become work-orientated at the expense of family ties to succeed. It is possible to imagine Ozu circa *Tokyo Story* yearning for his old neighbourhood of Fukagawa, as depicted in the cheerful but far from inconsequential *Passing Fancy*, wherein a single father and his son can happily exist in a slum neighbourhood providing the local brewery offers steady work and the after-hours scene at the nearby restaurant is sufficiently sociable. Circularity may have been a characteristic of Ozu's oeuvre, but in terms of his Tokyo stories, the effects of a resurgent economy ultimately made it impossible for him to go back to the beginning. ⁜

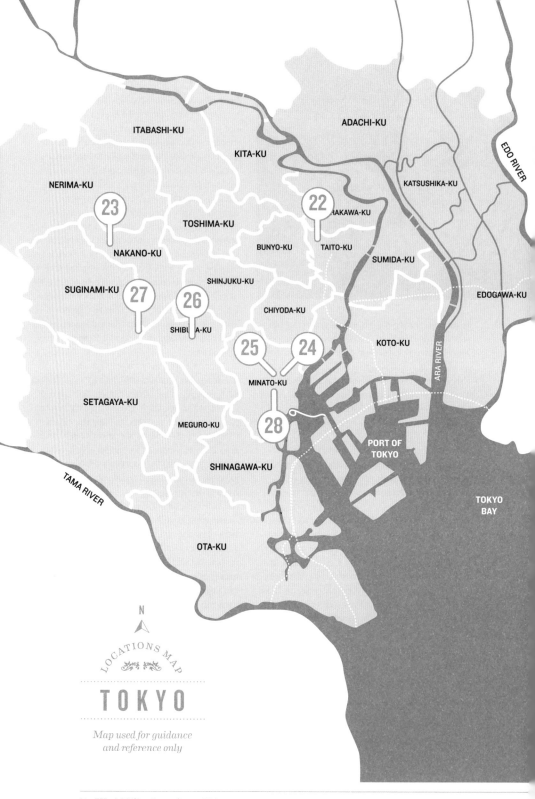

ITABASHI-KU

ADACHI-KU

KITA-KU

KATSUSHIKA-KU

EDO RIVER

NERIMA-KU

**23**

TOSHIMA-KU

**22**

ARAKAWA-KU

NAKANO-KU

BUNYO-KU

TAITO-KU

SUMIDA-KU

SUGINAMI-KU

**27**

SHINJUKU-KU

EDOGAWA-KU

**26**

CHIYODA-KU

SHIBUYA-KU

KOTO-KU

ARA RIVER

**25**

**24**

SETAGAYA-KU

MINATO-KU

**28**

MEGURO-KU

PORT OF
TOKYO

SHINAGAWA-KU

TOKYO
BAY

TAMA RIVER

OTA-KU

N

LOCATIONS MAP

# TOKYO

*Map used for guidance
and reference only*

# TOKYO LOCATIONS

## SCENES 22-28

# ENLIGHTENMENT GUARANTEED (1999)

LOCATION *Yanaka Cemetery, Yanaka 7-chome Taito*

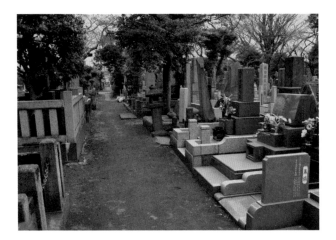

**FENG SHUI ADVISOR** Gustav has arrived in Japan from Germany with the intent of going on a spiritual retreat at a Buddhist monastery in Monzen on the Noto Peninsula. At the last minute, he is joined by his hapless brother Uwe, whose wife has just left him. At first, Gustav seems at ease on the streets of Tokyo armed with a book of pithy Zen words of wisdom instead of a map. However, after a night on the town, the brothers are unable to relocate their hotel. Their inability to communicate with the locals leads to them wandering aimlessly late into the night, eventually ending up in the Taito ward. Exhausted, they follow the example of the homeless people there by spending the night sleeping in cardboard boxes. Gustav and Uwe awake to find themselves in one of the Buddhist cemeteries next to the Tohoku Line. The tangle of railway lines and the un-swept autumn leaves work in this scene as metaphors for the brothers' spiritual state of mind. Sprawling cemeteries like Yanaka provide a welcome respite for Tokyoites from hectic city life. It is a popular place for walking and having picnics. Gustav appreciates the tranquility of waking in the cemetery, but Uwe is unimpressed. They are on separate but parallel paths in their spiritual journey towards enlightenment. This scene in the cemetery signals the beginning of the next phase of their journey in which they become separated from each other and need to rely upon their own wits. **•►Catherine Munroe Hotes**

(Photo ©Tomi Mäkitalo)

*Directed by Doris Dörrie*
**Scene description: Waking up in a cemetery in Taito Ward**
**Timecode for scene: 0:40:12 – 0:41:10**

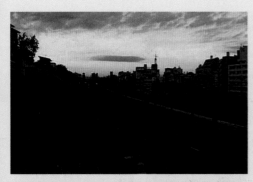 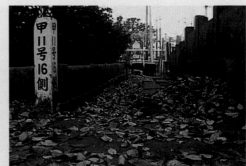

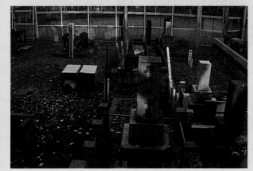 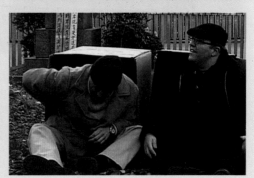

# CAFÉ LUMIÈRE (2003)

LOCATION *Tomaru Bookstore, 3-1-16, Koenji-Kita, Suginami-ku*

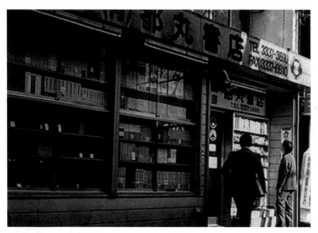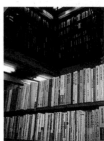

**CAFÉ LUMIÈRE** is an exquisite tribute to Yasujirô Ozu by the Taiwanese filmmaker Hou Hsiao-Hsien which was made to celebrate the centenary of Ozu's birth. Hou, like Ozu, is very much a master of the long take, with a similar preference for keeping his characters at a distance from the camera; this approach is evident in this sequence shot in Koenji, a lively shopping area that is one of the few parts of Tokyo that is still characteristic of the pre-1980s era. Young writer Yoko (Yo Hitoto) has discovered that she is pregnant, but considering her boyfriend to be too much of a mother's boy has decided to be a single mother, while continuing with her research project about the Taiwanese composer Jiang Wenge. It is this project that has brought her to the Tomaru Bookstore, where the volumes are piled high and the staff work quietly but efficiently; Yoko asks the manager if he knows anything about the composer, who was a frequent visitor to the store 60 or 70 years ago, but sadly he cannot help her. Exiting the store, Yoko walks through Koenji, making social arrangements with her friend by mobile phone as shoppers and residents pass by; Hou and cinematographer Lee Ping Bing capture the relaxed atmosphere of the area by gradually panning around, briefly losing sight of Yoko as if to emphasise that Café Lumière as much a film about the Tokyo of today as it is about the personal choices of the ostensible protagonist. **↝John Berra**

(Photo ©www.abaj.gr.jp/tomarushoten)

*Directed by Hou Hsiao-Hsien*
**Scene description: Researching and wandering in Koenji**
**Timecode for scene: 0:45:45 – 0:48:46**

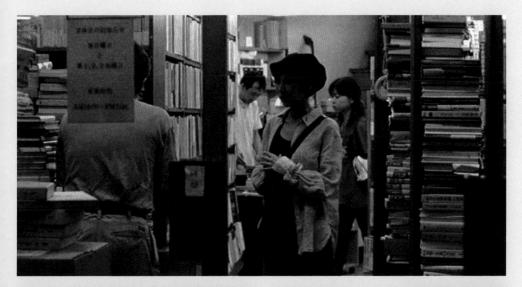

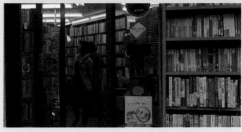 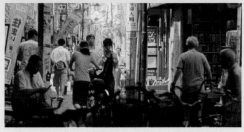

# FEAR AND TREMBLING (2003)

*NEC Supertower, 5-7-1 Shiba, Minato-ku*

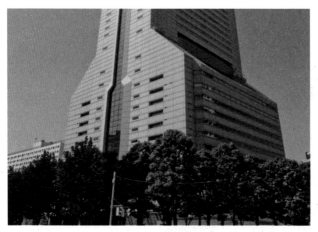
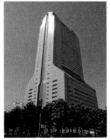

**MANY FOREIGN VISITORS** to Tokyo view the city as a maze of concrete and neon, but Amélie, the protagonist in Alain Corneau's 2003 French-Japanese co-production *Fear and Trembling*, finds herself navigating a different kind of maze. Hired on a year-long contract as a translator for the fictitious Yumimoto Corporation, Amélie (portrayed by French actress Sylvie Testud) finds herself lost in the complexities of Japanese social and corporate etiquette. Amélie is repeatedly disciplined and demoted by her sadistic superior, Fubuki-san (Kaori Tsuji) in this screen adaptation of Belgian author Amélie Nothomb's semi-autobiographical novel. The only thing that keeps Amélie sane throughout her descent to the bottom of the corporate ladder is a game she calls 'jumping out the window' in which she imagines herself falling off of the 44th floor of the Yumimoto Building and flying over Tokyo. The producers of the film cast the NEC Supertower in Minato-ku as the headquarters of Yumimoto. The 180-metre tall structure was constructed by the electronics giant in 1990 at the astounding cost of ¥60 billon, or just over $700 million. Ironically this construction coincided with the bursting of Japan's economic bubble and a decade later NEC would sell the building off. With some clever blue screen effects, Amélie uses the tower as her launching pad and does what so many visitors to Tokyo wish they could do – navigate the city from above as opposed to snaking though its notoriously maze-like streets. **⟿Chris MaGee**

(Photo ©Sergey Vladimirov)

*Directed by Alain Corneau*
**Scene description: Jumping out the window**
**Timecode for scene: 0:03:36 – 0:03:44**

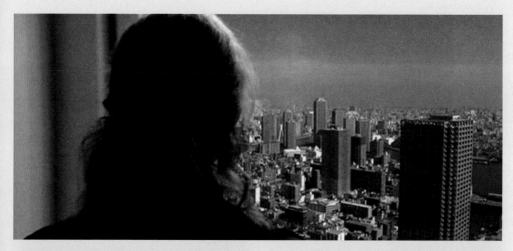

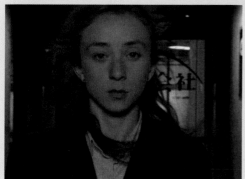
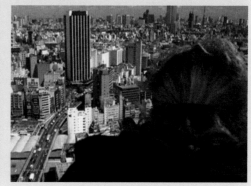

# KILL BILL VOLUME I (2003)

*Sound stage in Beijing (based on Gonpachi Restaurant, Nishi-Azabu)*

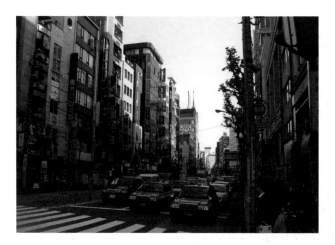

**QUENTIN TARANTINO'S** 2003 homage to Asian cult and Spaghetti Western cinema, *Kill Bill Volume 1*, is hardly the film to inspire any culinary choices. In fact, in the final scene, in which The Bride (Uma Thurman) surveys the battlefield and her violent handiwork on the minions of antagonist O-Ren Ishii (Lucy Liu), the opposite effect of making you lose your lunch might be achieved. However, beyond the incredible blood bath of this battle, also of marvel is the magnificent set-piece in which it took place, a lavish traditionally-themed Japanese restaurant. Though this final scene was shot on set, the design was greatly influenced by Gonpachi, a restaurant first constructed in 2001 in the upscale Tokyo neighborhood of Nishi-Azabu and designed to be an oasis of tradition smack dab in the center of modernity. Restaurants with a wide variety of interesting themes have been a part of the Tokyo dining experience since the Bubble Era. Take a 20 km ride up north from Nishi-Azabu to Gyoza Stadium in Ikebukuro, for example, and enjoy the varieties of gyoza sold there. Take the JR Yamanote to Shibuya for a drink at the twisted, haunted house-like Alcatraz ER. For those inclined toward the sacred, head in the opposite direction to Christon Café in Shinjuku with its garish Christian/gothic motifs. These restaurants, and many more, were born from a culture of both food obsession and just the need for a different sort dining experience to help unwind after a hard day at the office or kicking butt. **⇢Jon Jung**

Gonpachi Nishi-azabu, I-13-II Nishiazabu, Minato-ku

*Directed by Quentin Tarantino*
**Scene description: A foodie's fantasy world**
**Timecode for scene: 1:31:29 – 1:31:57**

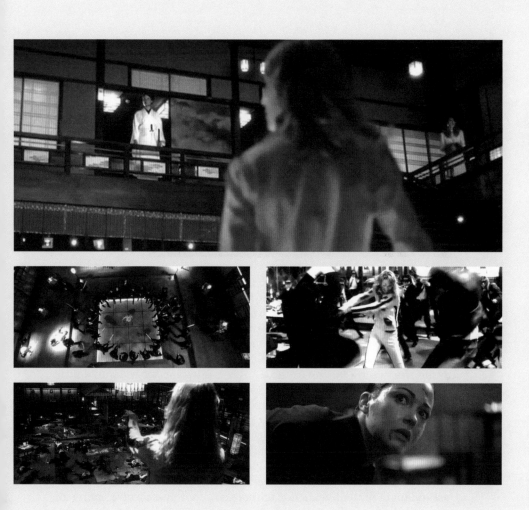

# LOST IN TRANSLATION (2003)

*An un-named Pachinko parlor in the Shibuya District*

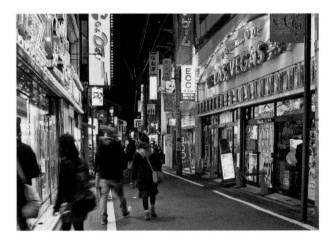

**SOFIA COPPOLA'S** 2003 film *Lost in Translation* is a classic 'fish out of water' scenario: Bob and Charlotte (Bill Murray and Scarlett Johansson) are strangers in a strange land who find solace in the company of each other. Director Sofia Coppola captured the feel of Tokyo, quirks and all and the city with its skyscrapers, flashing lights, and bustling crowds is just as much of a character in the film as Bob and Charlotte. In this scene, the two are fleeing from an angry bar owner, are separated from their group and duck into a pachinko parlor where they dart past various pachinko machines looking for an exit with the loud *pachin, pachin, pachin* of balls clacking on pins in the background. *Pachin* is the onomatopoeia that pachinko got its name from (the 'ko' is a word that refers to the ball itself). The game pachinko, normally thought to be uniquely Japanese, actually has its roots in the West. Pachinko is believed to be a variation on the French game bagatelle, itself a billiards variation and also an ascendant of pinball. At first, pachinko was merely a carnival game to win simple prizes like toys and candy, but now, pachinko is a 'grey' form of gambling and a multi billion yen business with TV commercials, commercial licenses and celebrities tied into its sub-industry. As in this scene and others in the film, pachinko parlors are ever-present in the modern Tokyo landscape. **↔Jon Jung**

**Above** Shibuya Street (Photo ©Miyuki Kobayashi)

*Directed by Sofia Coppola*
**Scene description: A midnight gamble**
*Timecode for scene: 0:46:23 – 0:46:48*

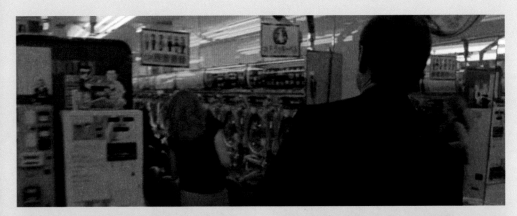

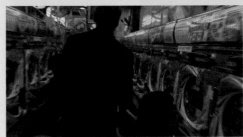
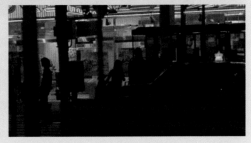

# NOBODY KNOWS (2002)

*Koenji Station, Suginami-ku*

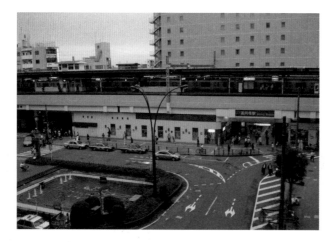

**TRAINS HOLD A PARTICULAR** fascination for many young boys
in Japan. Some can even mimic the station songs and recite the
announcements of their favourite route from memory. Though the trains
themselves hold feelings of exhilaration, for most Japanese children,
train stations symbolize the appearance and disappearance of their
commuting fathers. In Koreeda's film, it is a single mother whom the
children await. Inspired by an actual event, *Nobody Knows* depicts a
family of four children abandoned by their young working mother, a
child's eye view of survival in Tokyo. It is Yuki's birthday, probably her
fourth or fifth, and as a treat her eldest brother and stand-in parent Akira
takes her on an evening stroll to the station. *Nobody Knows* was filmed in
an outskirt of Shinjuku, with residential criss-cross streets overgrown
with canopies of electrical wires, but the location plays an anonymous
part in the film. They walk down a shopping lane where Yuki points as
she walks, 'tomato, daikon, broccoli, squash, carrots...' soaking up her
surroundings like a live-action picture book. This is the first time she's
left the apartment since they moved in a month ago. They stop to watch
the monorail train pass overhead (though it doesn't actually pass Koenji
station), and Akira promises to take her to Haneda airport to watch the
planes one day. It's the only gift he can offer her. •◦*Naomi Hocura*

(Photo ©Tyoron2)

Directed by Hirokazu Koreeda
**Scene description: Yuki's birthday**
**Timecode for scene: 1:08:26 – 1:10:11**

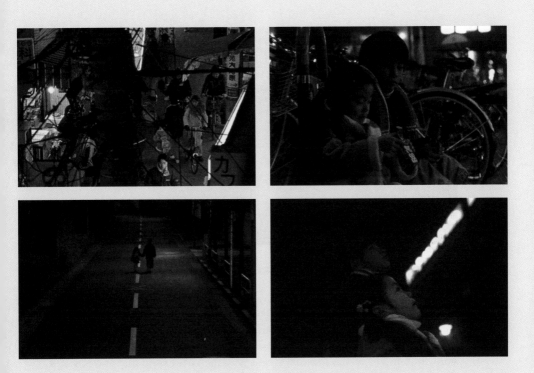

# ALWAYS: SUNSET ON THIRD STREET (2005)

*Atago, Minato-ku*

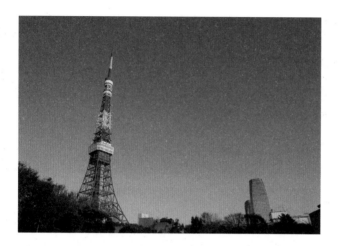

**ALWAYS: SUNSET ON THIRD STREET** was a smash in Japan, boasting blockbuster grosses and winning twelve Japan Academy Awards including Best Picture of 2005. Its wistfully nostalgic, heartfelt depiction of a small working-class neighbourhood in 1958 Tokyo caught the public's imagination in no small part due to the underlying optimism and *ganbatte* spirit of the film's characters, all of whom were struggling to find their place in a culture in flux. The narrow dirt street on which they lived may have lacked for glamour and comforts, but the Suzuki Auto family, writer Chagawa, and other residents knew one another by name and enjoyed a close-knit community more or less impossible in modern-day Tokyo. Though the film-makers have been smilingly vague, consensus among film-fan sleuths is that the neighbourhood, recreated through sets and CGI, is present-day Atago in Minato-ku; and based on the neighbourhood's proximity to and view of the then-under-construction Tokyo Tower in the title sequence, the children – among them young Kazuki Koshimizu as mischievous Ippei Suzuki – round the corner chasing their toy plane at Toranomo San-chome on Sakurada Dori. Minato-ku, the ward of Tokyo containing both Tokyo Tower and Roppongi, is now fabulously expensive real estate, but in 1958 was still recovering from the destruction, both literal and financial, of World War II. The Atago neighbourhood has a considerable number of shrines, temples and green spaces, making it a small but charming oasis amid the business and tourist bustle of this part of Tokyo. ➻*Eric Evans*

**Above** Tokyo tower and Atago green hills (Photo ©Orange Kuma)

*Directed by Takashi Yamazaki*
**Scene description: Chasing a toy plane through digital Tokyo**
**Timecode for scene: 0:02:35 – 0:03:50**

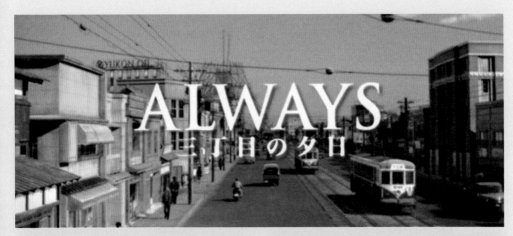

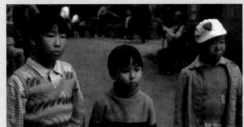
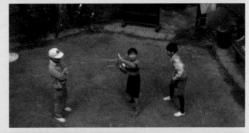

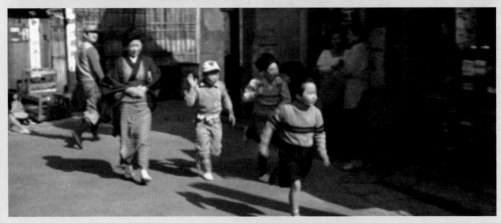

# STRANGERS AMONG US

Text by
ROBERTA
NOVIELLI

## A cinematic view of immigrants in Tokyo

**THE UNCEASING** migratory flux from various Asian countries to Japan, particularly to Tokyo, has been continuing from the end of World War II up until today, with a peak during the bubble economy of the 1980s. Recently, Japan's ageing population and low birthrate has stimulated a new need for foreign labour. It has been estimated that in 2007 foreign workers in Japan numbered about 2 million. This doesn't factor in illegal workers and residents, some of which constitute a conspicuous population of underground yakuza society.

Films portraying this 'alien world' in Tokyo represent one of the most interesting genres of the last four decades of Japanese cinema, starting with Nagisa Oshima's tragic *Death by Hanging* which told the true life story of a Korean man condemned to death for raping and murdering two Japanese girls. In the early 1990s Japanese film-makers took Oshima's example and transposed into their films the relatively recent multi-cultural

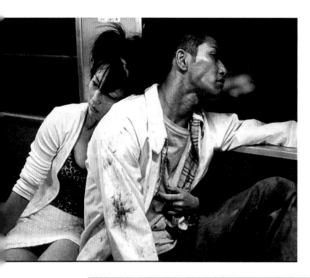

atmosphere of Tokyo. They especially focused on the individual dramas of foreigners in the capital, sympathizing with their sense of maladjustment and stressing the discriminatory attitude of Japanese toward them.

The first Japanese film-makers to seriously devote their work to this matter in the 1990s were in fact those of foreign ancestry. The *zainichi*, or ethnic Korean-Japanese film-maker Yoichi Sai, for example, has directed important views of the foreign experience in Japan. *All Under the Moon* (1993) uses light comedy to depict the ambiguous relationship between a Korean taxi driver and a Filipino woman navigating life in Tokyo, and his more recent *Blood and Bones* (2004) stars Takeshi Kitano as the brutal patriarch of a Korean family in Osaka. The hardships he and his children face are Sai's symbolic portrait of the whole Korean community of Japan.

Katsuhiro Otomo, best known for directing the anime blockbuster *Akira*, teased the plight of foreigners in Tokyo with an even more comedic sensibility in his live-action film *World Apartment Horror* (1991). The story, based on a manga by animator Satoshi Kon, follows a yakuza thug (Hiroyuki Tanaka) as he tries to scare a group of foreigners from Korea, India, the Philippines and China from a run down Tokyo apartment block... that also happens to be haunted!

A similar theme of a tightly-knit society of foreign residents makes up the center of *Swallowtail Butterfly* (Shunji Iwai, 1996). Fortune seekers from across Asia crowd into the fictional slums of Yentown on the outskirts of Tokyo where they do anything for cash, even founding their own rock band. The same de-homogenization and mood carries over into Masashi Yamamoto's bizarre comedy *Atlanta Boogie* (1996), where

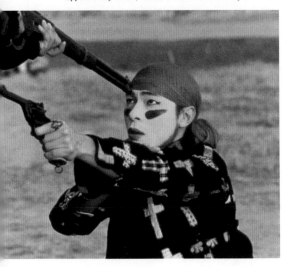

The only fulfilment in his empty everyday life is his love affair with Ailin, a Japanese woman of Chinese descent. He tries to change his precarious existence by robbing a local pachinko parlor, but he fails. Ho Jun feels he has no choice but to prostitute himself and to sell Ailin to the yakuza owner of the parlor. A mixture of death, sex, money and power paints a multi-racial fresco where human beings can only find escape through death, like cows in a slaughterhouse.

More and more radical representations of foreign residents in Tokyo have come to the screen in recent years, so as to stimulate a blend of cultures in Japanese film. Some would call it globalization, but others would call it a dystopic treatment of reality. In this sub-genre one name has prevailed – Takashi Miike. Miike creates a kind of axonometric projection of foreigners and Japanese living side-by-side in Tokyo. He uses splinters of violence, psychotropic images of solitude, dark comedic elements, and shredded morals to create impossible relationships. Tokyo's urban geography is criss-crossed by characters from all over the world – the '*zanryu koji*' ('orphans who have remained behind'), Chinese sons of Japanese war-time colonists who return to their homeland but never become integrated as real Japanese. They can't even feel nostalgic for their native country as their identity is transnational and their existence nomadic. It is impossible for them to dream of any future.

The shifting of national boundaries inside Tokyo thus challenges the idea of cultural identity. Reality is now seen as a hybrid among different cultural influences. The Japanese film industry is picking up this new trend by financing a growing amount of films co-produced with other Asian countries. An example of this is the 2010 screen adaptation of the seminal novel by Haruki Murakami, *Norwegian Wood*. This book is considered by Japanese people as one of the 'sacred fruits' of Tokyo, but as a reflection of these new ideas of cultural identity Tokyo-based production company Asmik Ace selected not a Japanese film-maker, but the French-Vietnamese director Tran Anh Hung, whose sensual style definitely makes the love story a transnational myth. ✦

strangers compete with Japanese people in a local sports challenge traditionally intended for residents as a symbol of the Japanese spiritual values. One year later, Yamamoto's viewpoint of foreigners took a bitter turn. *Junk Food* (1997) tells various slice of life stories set in a sordid Tokyo, including one that centres around a an Esat Indian man who in a jealous rage kills his Japanese girlfriend.

Some films from the 1990s touched on how the situation for foreign women in Tokyo can be far worse than their male counterparts. One of these films, *Where Hot Tears Overflow* (Tashiro Hirotaka, 1992) tells of a Filipina mail-order bride who faces the tragic situation of divorcing her Japanese husband only to crash headlong into discrimination and social alienation.

One of the ultimate Japanese outsiders is the young Chinese immigrant of *About love, Tokyo* (Mitsuo Yanagimachi, 1992). Ho Jun lives with other Chinese friends in a small dormitory. All of them share the fact that in Japan they belong nowhere. Ho Jun works in a slaughterhouse, unable to escape the desperate glances of the animals he kills.

**Films portraying this 'alien world' in Tokyo represent one of the most interesting genres of the last four decades of Japanese cinema**

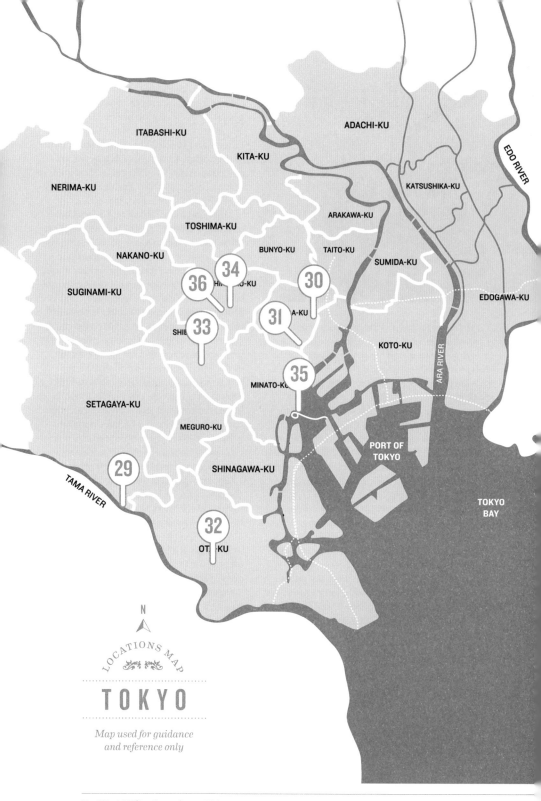

ITABASHI-KU

KITA-KU

ADACHI-KU

EDO RIVER

NERIMA-KU

KATSUSHIKA-KU

TOSHIMA-KU

ARAKAWA-KU

NAKANO-KU

BUNYO-KU

TAITO-KU

**36** **34** H...O-KU

**30**

SUMIDA-KU

SUGINAMI-KU

**31** A-KU

EDOGAWA-KU

**33** SHI...

KOTO-KU

ARA RIVER

**35**

SETAGAYA-KU

MINATO-KU

MEGURO-KU

PORT OF
TOKYO

TOKYO
BAY

**29** SHINAGAWA-KU

TAMA RIVER

**32** OT...KU

N

LOCATIONS MAP

TOKYO

*Map used for guidance
and reference only*

# TOKYO LOCATIONS

## SCENES 29-36

# NANA (2005)

LOCATION

*Un-named apartment overlooking the Tama River*

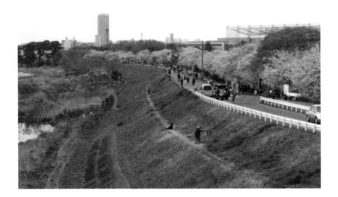

**THE TAMA RIVER** cuts a wide swath through Honshu with its eastern reaches forming a natural border between Tokyo and Kanagawa. As the river is very prone to flooding, a berth of parkways lines its shores. For many decades, the Tama River has been a place for city dwellers to enjoy a respite from the crowded city streets of central Tokyo. The river plays a significant role in Ai Yazawa's wildly popular *Nana* manga series which Kentaro Otani adapted into a hit live action film in 2005. Many important scenes occur in the series when characters are walking along the Tama River, either in small groups or to reflect alone about the difficult circumstances that life throws their way. In this scene, both Nanas are brought for the first time to Room 707 – the apartment that they will soon share. This slightly worn, European-style apartment overlooking the Tama River symbolizes the friendship between the main protagonists: punk rocker Nana Osaki and the super-kawaii Nana 'Hachi' Komatsu. There are numerological signs that indicate the importance of the room: the girls share the name Nana, which is a homonym for the number 7. From this seventh floor apartment, they enjoy an idyllic view of the Tama River. Otani has romanticized the view by using soft focus. The contrast between the hard-as-nails Nana and the sweet, trusting Hachi is reflected in the contrast of urban and rural landscapes. **◆Catherine Munroe Hotes**

**Above** On the banks of the Tama River (Photo ©f.masaru, Panoramio)

*Directed by Kentaro Otani*

**Scene description: The two Nanas discover apartment 707 on the Tama River**
**Timecode for scene: 0:12:56 – 0:15:45**

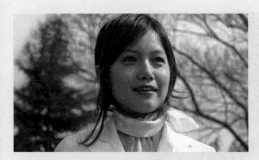 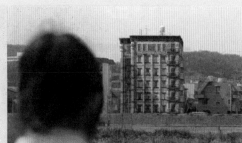

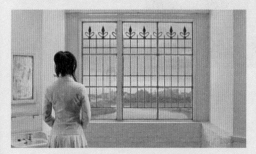 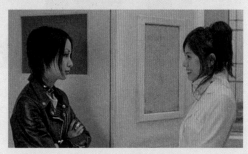

# TRAIN MAN/DENSHA OTOKO (2005)

LOCATION *Akihabara Electric Town, 1-12-1 Soto-Kanda Chiyoda-ku*

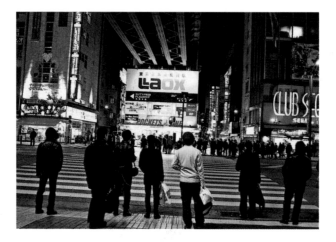

**AKIHABARA, OR 'AKIBA'** for short, is the place of electronic dreams.
Located squarely at the three o'clock position on the Yamanote train loop,
Akihabara, and more specifically its 'Electric Town' area has offered
the most popular electronic items of each era and every component and
part you could possibly think of. During and after World War II, radios
were the hot item. Then, in the following decades of the burgeoning
middle class, home appliances were the trend. As the information age
was introduced in the 1970s and continued to present day, computers
and software have been Akihabara's specialties. Another more modern
trend in Akihabara have been products and services catering to *otaku*, a
subculture best described as obsessive hobbyists. With items including
manga and anime tie-in products, maid cafes and massive multi-floor
arcades, Akihabara's cultural influence is currently being felt around the
world. Even wielding such influence, *otaku* are still seen as nerds and
geeks. *Train Man*, a 2005 otaku-meets-girl comedy, starts with several
scenes shot in Akihabara, the 'hang out' spot for the film's *otaku* and
computer geek protagonist. Shots included are a wide shot of the Japan
Railways overpass over Kuramae Hashi Dori, storefronts and their neon
signs, crowds walking by, an *otaku* retrieving a capsule toy, all ending
in a shot of the film's protagonist walking into a store to covet an anime
figurine. You would almost expect Jacques Cousteau to narrate this
opening scene with, 'This is the otaku in its natural habitat.' ➼*Jon Jung*

(Photo ©Miyuki Kobayashi)

*Directed by Shosuke Murakami*
**Scene description: Walking the neon streets of Akihabara**
**Timecode for scene: 0:00:45 – 0:01:10**

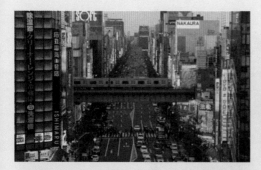 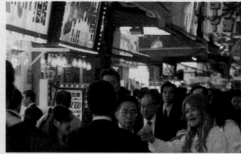

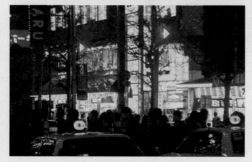 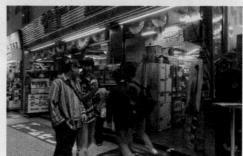

# CONFESSIONS OF A DOG (2006)

LOCATION *The Foreign Correspondents' Club of Japan, Yurakucho Denki North Building 20F Yurakucho 1-7-1, Chiyoda-ku*

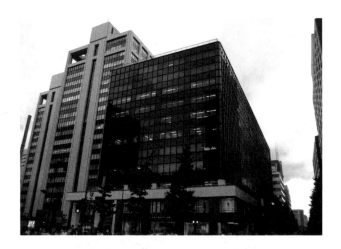

**THE MAJORITY OF LOCATIONS** in this book are easily accessible to any tourist or Tokyoite, but there are some that few in Japan's capital ever get to see, at least in person. One of these locales is the Foreign Correspondents' Club of Japan. The irony is that this private club for journalists, photographers and writers living in Japan is probably one of the most public locations in the city. The Club, founded in November 1945, has played host to Japanese heads of state, corporate executives, authors and more than a few famous film stars. All have used the Club as a podium from which to speak to the world. If you watch a news broadcast from Tokyo, chances are you'll be seeing the Foreign Correspondents' Club on the twentieth floor of the Yurakucho Denki North Building. You can also see the Club in Gen Takahashi's controversial 2006 film *Confessions of a Dog*. Takahashi sets one of the climactic scenes of his over three-hour exposé of corruption in Japanese law enforcement in the Club's main conference room. After having suffered through intimidation and violence, freelance journalist Kusama (Junichi Kawamoto) and photographer Kitamura (Kunihiko Iida) blow the lid on the polices' lawlessness in a press conference. As Kusama says (through a translator), 'To describe the Japanese police force in one word would use the word *bōryokudan*, or gangster.' This triumphant moment is undercut when we're shown Sergeant Nara (Taisei Miyamoto), a drug-addicted cop whose crimes have landed him behind bars. ➼ *Chris MaGee*

**Above** Denki Building

*Directed by Gen Takahashi*
**Scene description: Blowing the lid off police corruption**
*Timecode for scene: 2:43:28 – 2:49:18*

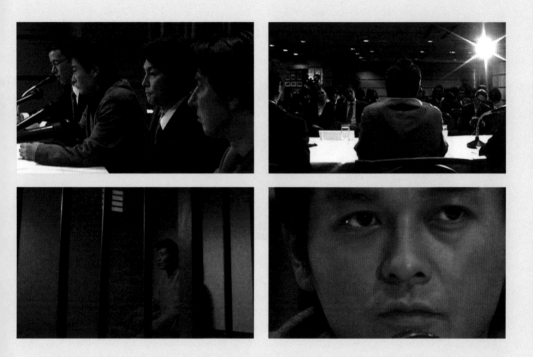

# IT'S ONLY TALK/YAWARAKAI SEIKATSU (2006)

LOCATION *Kamata Tokyu Plaza Amusement Park, Kamata Tokyu*

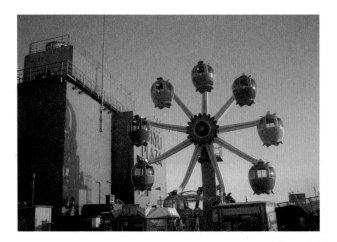

**AFTER A PRE-ARRANGED** rendezvous with a sexually-repressed salaryman in a darkened cinema, unattached 35-year-old Yuko takes in an unfamiliar swathe of city from a mall rooftop in dreary Kamata. 'This is an odd place. Not like Tokyo at all,' she says to her polite groper. He explains that Kamata was where the old Shochiku film studios stood and that perverts favour out-of-the-way movie theatres. 'I wonder if I should move here,' she replies. Over this wide shot of grey, urban sprawl Yuko's journey of discovery begins. A Ferris wheel carriage rises like a space capsule, with Yuko as its astronaut. Inside, she snaps photos of her newly decided home. The mini-Ferris wheel slowly turns in the deep blue sky of magic hour. Its Tokyu Plaza rooftop location epitomizes frivolous amusements built en-masse during the latter half of Japan's hopeful Showa-era, now imbued with the patina of a bygone time. Yuko then strolls along the tracks of the JR Keihin-Tohoku line which shuttles commuters down to Ofuna, Kanagawa (former site of another Shochiku studio). Next is Kamata's *pièce de résistance* – an old playground fashioned from used tyres. She marvels at the towering rubber dinosaur at its centre. This opening sequence perfectly captures the sensation of discovering a new world in your backyard. Yuko is entranced by starting a new life in a place 'without an ounce of chic.' We soon find out that this initial high is one of the ups and downs of Yuko's crushing depression. ➥*Jason Gray*

**Above** Ferris wheel at Tokyu Plaza Amusement Park (Photo ©niima)

*Directed by Ryuichi Hiroki*

**Scene description: Yuko discovers the Tokyo suburb of Kamata**
**Timecode for scene: 0:03:15 – 0:06:33**

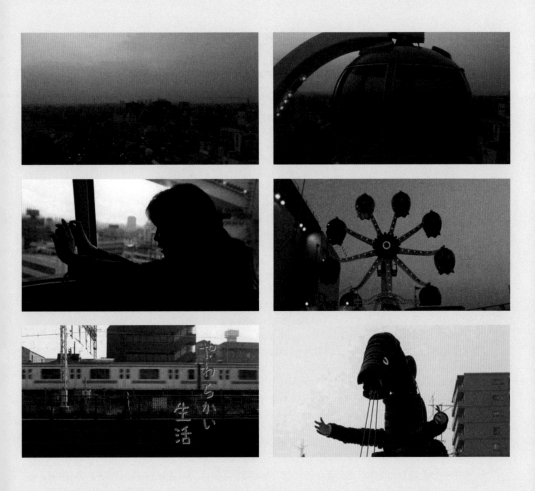

# BABEL (2006)

LOCATION

*The J-Pop Café, Shibuya Beam 7F. 31-2 Udagawa-cho, Shibuya-ku*

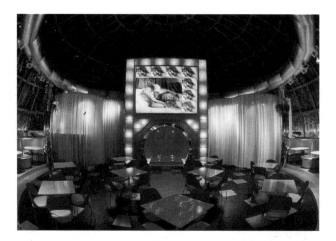

**ARGUABLY THE MOST** aesthetically invigorating story strand of Alejandro González Iñárritu's global commentary *Babel* takes place in Tokyo, with the city being captured from the point of view of Chieko (Rinko Kikuchi), a deaf teenage girl who is struggling to deal with both sexual frustration and the suicide of her mother. Seeking escape from her increasingly difficult relationship with her father Yasujiro (Kōji Yakusho), Chieko meets up with her friends at the J-Pop Café, a sprawling – and sexualised – hangout for upwardly mobile teenagers located on the 7th floor of a building in Shibuya. The venue is divided into several areas, and Iñárritu's constantly moving camera provides a vividly realised tour that takes in pop culture reference points to a Japanese youth movement that has filtered the influence of Westernisation through its own sense of style. Chieko meets her friends in the dining section of the cafe, where she makes eye contact with a fashionable youth, then ventures into the arcade area where the boy is encouraged by his crew to make his move, only to lose interest once he learns that Chieko is, in fact, impaired. The sequence is accompanied by a loud sugar-rush of electronic J-pop that perfectly complements the excitable behavior of Chieko and her friends; however, this teenage playground takes on a darker dimension when the rejected Chieko flashes her crotch in a sexual display of teenage insouciance on her way out of the building, much to the shock of both her friends and the disinterested suitor. ➻ *John Berra*

*Directed by Alejandro González Iñárritu*
**Scene description: Youth in revolt at the J-Pop Café**
**Timecode for scene: 0:22:13 – 0:26:21**

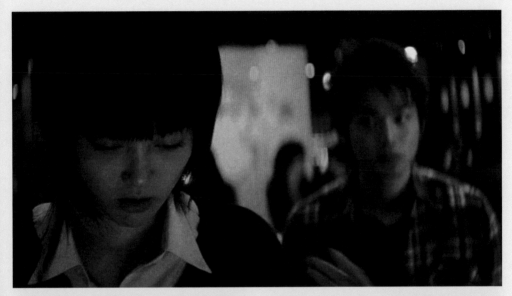

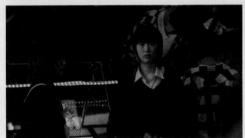
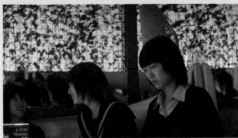

# NUANCE (2006)

*Green Peas Pachinko Parlor, 3-36-1 Shinjuku, Shinjuku-ku*

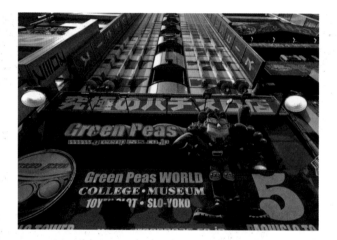

**IN 2006,** the Tokyo film-makers' collective Image Forum commissioned sixteen Japanese artists to create animated shorts inspired by the city of Tokyo. The project was called 'Tokyo Loop' and the shorts were all scored by the renowned underground musician Seiichi Yamamoto. The resulting films varied from comical vignettes to abstract impressions of the city. Tomoyasu Murata chose to hit the streets of Tokyo armed with his camera in order to photograph the urban landscapes and movements of the city. The film opens and closes with the densely packed cityscape of central Tokyo filling the screen. Murata's initial photographs captured the frenetic movement of traffic through the streets of Tokyo, but the landscapes and people seemed colourless and boring. So, he altered the photographs by colouring or painting over them. He opens the film with a montage that emphasizes the architectural structures and the movement of traffic passing through the city. After a painted streetscape of Shinjuku, Murata fills the screen with streaks of paint and shifts to a more contemplative mood. The image was layered first with coloured crayons, then obscured with black crayon. He then scratched through the black with a toothpick to reveal the colours below. The result is a beautiful impression of Tokyo's neon lit streets at night and the constant flow of people through the city using various forms of transportation. As the title suggests, *Nuance* is an animated experiment at subtly expressing the director's emotional response to the city that is his home. ⮞*Catherine Munroe Hotes*

(Photo ©qjphotos)

*Directed by Tomoyasu Murata*
**Scene description: Tokyo abstracted**
**Timecode for scene: 0:00:53 – 0:02:43**

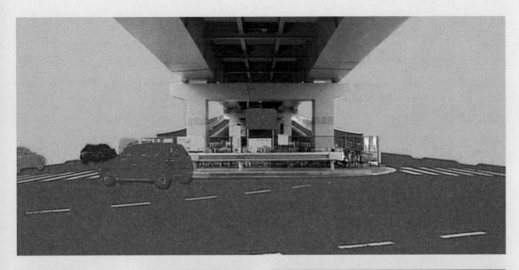

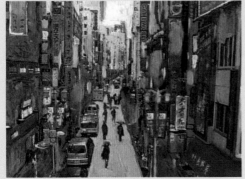 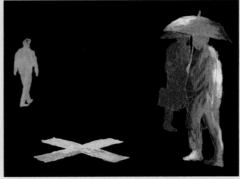

# RETRIBUTION (2006)

LOCATION *Rainbow Bridge, 3-33-19 Kaigan, Minato-ku*

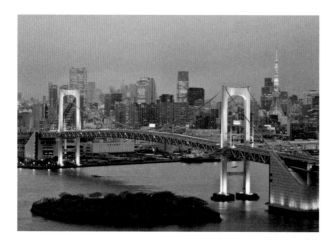

**BEING SIX CENTURIES OLD,** Tokyo is bound to have a few ghosts lurking about. In Kiyoshi Kurosawa's supernatural mystery *Retribution,* a restless spirit rises from the foundations of Tokyo's redeveloped waterfront to haunt homicide detective Noboru Yoshioka. The detective finds himself under suspicion of murder after evidence connects him to a drowned woman found in a landfill site along Tokyo Bay. Yoshioka has no memory of the crime, but he still finds himself tormented by visions of the murder victim, identified only as F18. One overcast afternoon as Yoshioka walks the crime scene at the foot of The Rainbow Bridge he is confronted by F18's ghost. The terror jolts a memory from his subconscious – an abandoned building that stood on the waterfront fifteen years before. How are this woman and this building connected? In the late 1980s Tokyo's waterfront Odaiba district began to be reshaped into a futuristic community dubbed Tokyo Teleport Town. Buildings were demolished and tons of landfill was poured into the Bay. Before developers could move people in though, the bottom fell out of the Japanese economy. It would take years before this area of the city would live up to its original potential, but you couldn't tell that from Retribution. 'A disappointment' is what Yoshioka calls his bayside home. This post-Bubble gloom permeates the film as Yoshioka digs down, decade upon decade, into the muddy landscape beneath the Rainbow Bridge and Odaiba in order to unearth this woman's true identity. ➺*Chris MaGee*

**Above** Tokyo's Rainbow Bridge seen from Fuji TV Observation tower (Photo ©Sam Gao)

*Directed by Kiyoshi Kurosawa*
*Scene description: The ghost of F18 confronts Detective Yoshioka*
*Timecode for scene: 0:49:07 – 0:51:42*

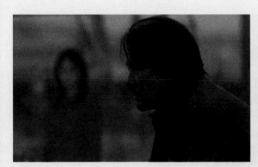 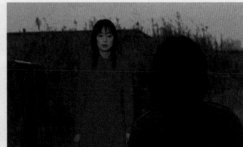

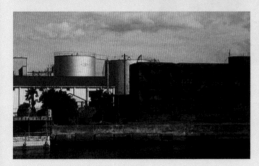 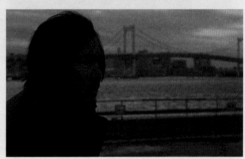

# ADRIFT IN TOKYO (2007)

LOCATION *Shinjuku*

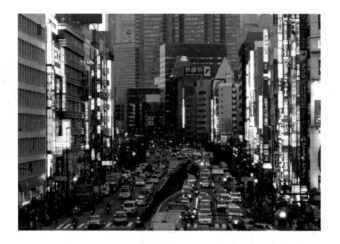

**MORE THAN ANY OTHER** area in Tokyo, Shinjuku embodies everything that gives the city its inimitable identity. Shinjuku Station is the city's symbolic heart, with over 3.5 million people passing through it every day. Spiraling out from the station, the sinuous and asymmetrical streets lead to every imaginable and unimaginable desire that the city has to offer. One path leads to the dark pleasures of Kabuki-cho, another to the labyrinthine bookshop Kinokukiya, one to the public spectacle of cosplay in Yoyogi Park, another to the long-standing underground live house called Theater Poo. Even after passing through the station regularly, one wrong turn means ending up lost in another completely unknown Tokyo. Appropriately it is here that Fumiya, the directionless protagonist of *Adrift in Tokyo*, finds himself enchanted by a strange wandering glam guitarist and follows him through the endless wonderland of Shinjuku. Although the dayglo guitarist seems a little far-fetched, anyone who has visited Tokyo knows that one has to suspend disbelief while in the city, as if watching a film. As Fumiya follows his musical muse, he becomes a *flâneur* in the truest sense, giving himself over completely to the city. Up until this point in the film Fumiya had been wandering the city only as a way of eradicating his debt to Fukuhara, his loan shark, but it is only here, with no motives other than curiosity and joy, that he is able to genuinely and fully experience life. ➼ *Brandon Hocura*

**Above** Koshu Kaido neon, Shinjuku (Photo ©Chris Jongkind)

*Directed by Miki Satoshi*
**Scene description: Glam wanderer**
*Timecode for scene: 0:53:50 – 0:56:57*

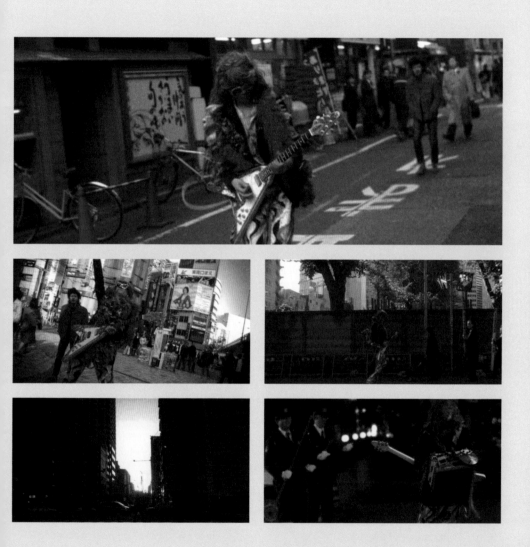

# SHINJUKU

*Dawn is wet*

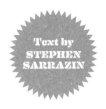

Text by
STEPHEN
SARRAZIN

**SHINJUKU IS THE PLACE** in Tokyo where dreams measure up. The most celebrated area of the city, along with Shibuya, Shinjuku exists as a rhizomatic network of histories and mythologies, its labyrinthian train station still the busiest in the world. From the strip clubs and gambling parlors of Kabukicho, to the counter-culture bars and cafés that make up Golden Gai. This is where artists and intellectuals have gathered for decades, the site an enduring shrine to continental longings and home to perhaps the most famous film loving bar, La Jetée. From Okubo, Tokyo's Korean district, to Shinjuku Ni-Chome, its gay quarter, Shinjuku overflows with tales ready for the taking. A place simultaneously international and intensely Japanese; streets and establishments found in Kabukicho, the red light district, are not always as tourist-friendly as Paris' Pigalle. It has retained an edge once associated with New York's Time Square, with a touch of 1970s squalor.

Yet Shinjuku's main avenues teem with luxury hotels and department stores, as well as the Tokyo Metropolitan Government Building, an example of what the future used to look like.

In spite of its diversity of means, people and politics, Shinjuku is linked by a trait distinguishing it from Tokyo's other wards: its unsentimentality. Shinjuku is for grown-ups, or a place to grow up fast. Neither cute nor soft nor sweet, it provides balance to an odd sense of aging angst permeating other parts of the city. Shinjuku navigates between the destitute and the epic.

It is a Shangri-la of psycho-geography, a Situationist's dream come true, the landscape of hundreds of films, including some of Japanese cinema's modern and contemporary masterpieces. Such as Nagisa Oshima's *Diary of a Shinjuku Thief, the story of Birdie and Umeko*, set against the backdrop of the 1968 Zengakuren demonstrations against American bases in

Japan, which mirrored the Paris of May. The means to express this protest included politics, intellect and sexuality, combined in a narrative that sees a young book thief caught in the act by a young woman in a Shinjuku bookstore, who embark on a quest that embraces all appetites. Their passionate escapade through the maze of Shinjuku streets recalls the vibrant and kinetic energy of Jean-Luc Godard's rebels in *Breathless* (1960), a constant model for Oshima. The great director would invest himself in a decade of radical and provocative film-making that would take him to France in the late 1970s to find financing for his *Empire of the Senses* and back to the safety of shooting on sets. Oshima made Shinjuku feel European.

For the great studio Nikkatsu's working-class intellectuals, its writers and directors, Shinjuku in the early 1970s became a reservoir of possibilities. Directors would boldly send their actors among the crowd, performing the most outlandish acts, wearing revealing attire, to the awe, amusement and occasional fear of involuntary extras, seizing everything as if a documentary crew, with over the shoulder camera shots and movements, capturing sounds of the streets, before the voices of the performers would be dubbed in.

Noboru Tanaka, a former assistant to Shohei Immamura and Seijun Suzuki, an admirer of French surrealist poetry, directed one of Nikkatsu's finest 'Shinjuku women' films, a world away from the male yakuza violence of other genre pictures. *Night of the Felines* (1972) looks at a season in the lives of two young women working at a 'soapland', Masako and Jun, the latter pointing to the generation ahead while the former carries that glimmer of counterculture associated with Tokyo at the time, as when Masako encounters an absurdist performance by a man

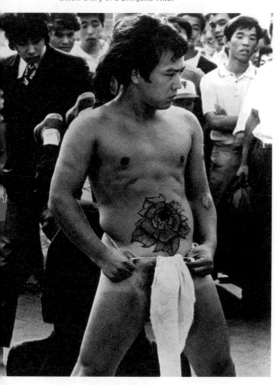

and woman on a train track involving a deck chair, an umbrella and a gold fish.

Tanaka's surrealist parenthesis evokes that brief period when Japanese art was in synch with international contemporary culture and activism, when it still held political aspirations, exemplified by the students and unions' strikes of the late 1960s up to 1970, which Oshima captured in his film. But by the time Tanaka sets his felines loose, Japan has turned an economic corner, has achieved prosperity and is less than a decade away from the dizzying wealth of the bubble years.

The director does not celebrate nor condemn the lives of these two women, but rather transforms Kabukicho and its surroundings into an odd community. Masako remains lucid and can sense a new tide wading in. In one of the most Antonionian sequences found in Japanese cinema, one that rivals the film art of Kiju Yoshida, Tanaka shows us Masako and her lover exiting onto the streets of Shinjuku at dawn after a final night of passion that leads them to unexpected choices and cumbersome romance.

Watching the sun come up over the Keio department store entrance on the west side of Shinjuku station, the man falls to the ground while a cleaning truck from the city, seen from the point of view of a face resting on the curb, turns on the water to wash away the night trash while the surrounding shops, in a stunning montage of noisily rising grids, get ready for business. Tanaka made Shinjuku Japanese all over again.

Threading a fine line between Oshima and Tanaka was Shuji Terayama, writer/poet/playwright, director, gambler and a distant cousin to film artists Jean Eustache and Pier Paolo Pasolini, whose work was linked to both European avant-garde and Japanese counterculture. In his seminal film *Throw Away your Books, Go into the Streets*, a jobless young man, Watashi/I, sets out on a Tokyo odyssey: a collage of encounters ranging from abuse and insults from members of a soccer team, to his first encounter with a prostitute while having to suffer his own dysfunctional family. The vision of Shinjuku offered here sheds a harsh light on a forbidden landscape used to shadows. Terayama aptly navigates a limbo located between beauty and decay. Watashi provokes the audience in an opening monologue, daring it to take to the streets, just as he closes the film, asking for the lights to be turned on, surrounded by cast and crew, having made it back home, the hearth of the culture.

When Shohei Immamura's former assistant-director Takashi Miike set foot in Shinjuku, in 1995 with *Shinjuku Triad Society*, the aspirations of Oshima and Terayama and the knowing innocence of Tanaka, are all gone. Shinjuku's backstreets become the turf where battles are fought between Japanese and Chinese crime mobs with the police trying to rival the brutality of each side. Miike, who would reinvent cinematic violence, combines the grotesque with the virtuoso, as Sam Peckinpah and John Woo had done before him – pushing the Shinjuku boundaries beyond 'hardboiled' and making it 'noir', where codes, rules, and traditions do little to cement warring factions. Honour is not in the books to begin with. The sadistic detective leading the film's investigation wishes solely to extract his lawyer-brother from the yakuza and fights Shinjuku's firm grip on him. Such is the lure of Shinjuku. ✦

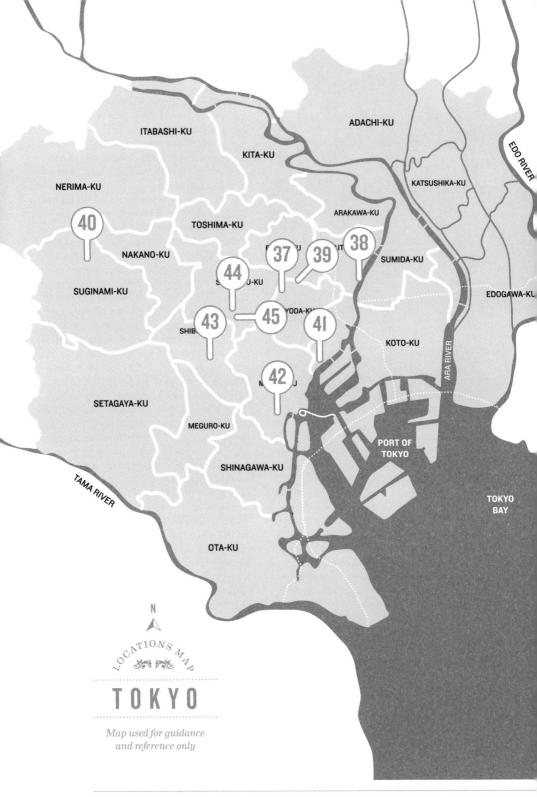

ITABASHI-KU

KITA-KU

ADACHI-KU

EDO RIVER

NERIMA-KU

KATSUSHIKA-KU

TOSHIMA-KU

ARAKAWA-KU

**40**

NAKANO-KU

**37** **39** **38**

SUMIDA-KU

SUGINAMI-KU

**44**

SHINJUKU-KU

EDOGAWA-KU

**43** **45**

CHIYODA-KU

SHIB

**41**

KOTO-KU

**42**

ARA RIVER

SETAGAYA-KU

MEGURO-KU

PORT OF TOKYO

SHINAGAWA-KU

TOKYO BAY

TAMA RIVER

OTA-KU

N

LOCATIONS MAP

# TOKYO

*Map used for guidance and reference only*

# TOKYO LOCATIONS

## SCENES 37-45

# YASUKUNI (2007)

LOCATION *Yasukuni Shrine, 3-1-1 Kudan-kita Chiyoda-ku*

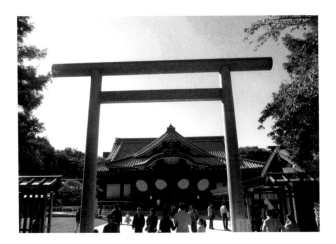

**15 AUGUST 2005.** A man in his seventies comes to pay homage at Yasukuni Shrine. He waits at the gate for it to open, a Japanese flag held above him. When the gates open, the camera follows him through the colossal *torii* that leads to the hall of worship. Director Ying Li spent ten years filming scenes like this, trying to objectively decide if Yasukuni Shrine is just a place of Shinto worship, or rather a façade hiding a sense of nostalgia for imperialism. Yasukuni Shrine is set in the heart of Tokyo, close to the Imperial Palace. Built in 1869 by order of Emperor Meiji, it hosts the souls of Japanese soldiers who died in service of the Emperor, together with those belonging to Japanese colonies. The families of the latter have repeatedly asked to remove them from the list of 'glorious spirits', but to no avail. From 1959 to 1978 the registry included 1,068 convicted war criminals. Shrine officials say these souls, or *kami*, deserve to be worshipped since they died for their country. Asian countries, who suffered Japanese brutality during World War II have fiercely protested against this inclusion, blaming Japan for its denial of war responsibilities. Nevertheless, former prime minister Jun'ichiro Koizumi never missed the chance to pay homage at Yasukuni, stating that it was not a political but a religious matter. Screenings in Tokyo were delayed because of threats from right wing nationalists; *Yasukuni* was finally screened in May 2008 under tight police security. **Jacopo Acqua**

(Photo ©Alex Trueman)

*Directed by Ling Yi*
*Scene description: An early morning worshipper*
*Timecode for scene: 0:05:42 – 0:09:41*

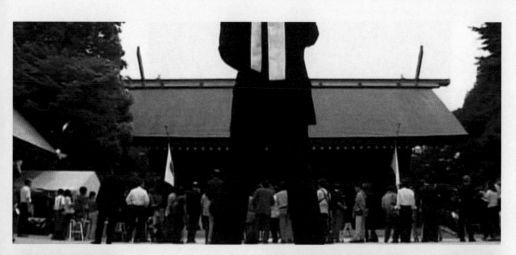

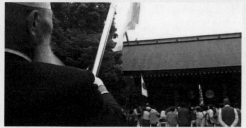

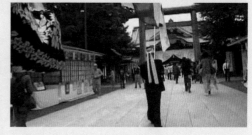

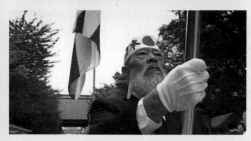

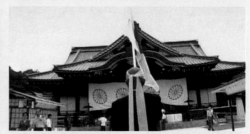

# BUY A SUIT (2008)

*Azumabashi Bridge, Sumida Koen Park, Sumida-ku*

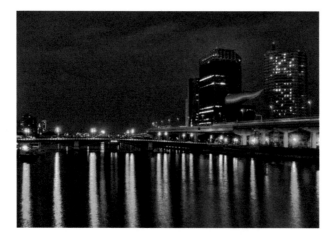

**JUN ICHIKAWA** has often taken as the subject of his films the city of
Tokyo and the lives of its inhabitants. *Buy a Suit*, unfortunately his last
work, was finished on the day of his death. Shot with a normal camcorder
and using only non-professional actors, the movie tells the story of Yuki
and her trip to Tokyo in search of her missing brother Hisashi – the only
information about him being a postcard he had sent and an address
written on it. Yuki starts her search near Azumabashi, a bridge located in
the Sumida ward, the central area where, among other things, the Tokyo
Sky Tree is now being constructed. When she begins to walk toward
the zone under the bridge, the action cuts to the countless blue tents set
along the Sumida river, the typical and recognizable cardboard shelters
built by the Japanese homeless population all over the country. Yuki
walks toward one of these blue tents. There a homeless man is leaving his
'house' as he busies himself with pots and coughs heavily. It is Hisashi,
her brother. The contrast between the shiny building and the seemingly
happy people walking through Tokyo and this community of blue tents,
which houses almost a different type of humanity, is depicted here in all
its simplicity. There's no dramatic intent in Ichikawa's shots; everything
is filmed as in a documentary or, to put it better, as in a home video. It is
what makes this scene, and film, so effective. ➜*Matteo Boscarol*

(Photo ©KortownExpress)

*Directed by Jun Ichikawa*
**Scene description: The discovery of the homeless community**
*Timecode for scene: 0:14:27 – 0:14:54*

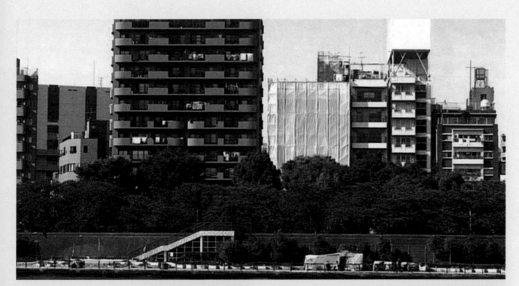

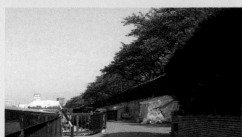
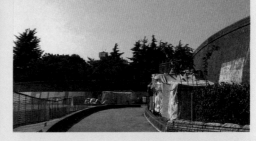

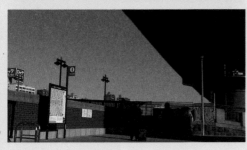
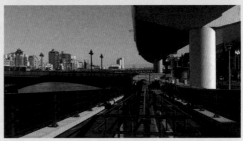

Images ©2008 Jun Ichikawa Office

# FINE, TOTALLY FINE (2008)

LOCATION *Unspecified used bookstore Jiibo-cho, Chiyoda-ku*

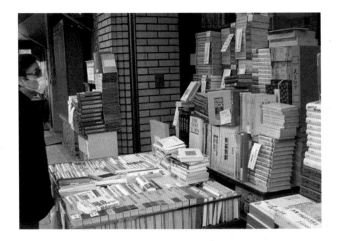

**JUST A STONE'S THROW** from five Tokyo universities lies the crossing of Yasukuni-dori and Hakusan-dori in Tokyo's Chiyoda ward. This intersection marks the center of Jinbo-cho, unofficial used-book capital of Japan. For several blocks, dozens of used bookstores are piled atop one another, home to literally millions of titles old and new. If a book exists, in print or not, you're likely to find it here. Down any side alley of this bibliophile's wonderland are smaller used bookshops and stalls. *Fine, Totally Fine*'s used bookstore set is a fair representation of the Japanese norm, featuring books from floor to ceiling on shelves built to maximize every available square inch of retail space. It's here that quiet, clumsy Akari (Kimura Yoshino) gets a job working for Teruo (YoshiYoshi Arakawa), a bookseller's son who is 30 going on 13. His crush on her notwithstanding, she meets a kindred soul in Yuhara (Naoki Tanaka), one of the shop's regular customers. He offers to buy a piece of the pastel art adorning the walls – her work – yet she demurs. She regrets the decision, and races through the neighbourhood to find him. The film boasts some of contemporary Japanese cinema's most peculiar characters, whose misadventures in life and love make for deadpan comedy. It also excels at showing a Tokyo not often seen on film, a part of town removed from the *Blade Runner* neon of the Ginza and Shinjuku where quiet lives intersect among walls seemingly built of books. **•◆Eric Evans**

**Above** One of the many used book stores in Jonbo-cho (Photo ©curzon@cominganarchy.com)

*Directed by Yosuke Fujita*
*Scene description: The bookstores and back streets of Jinbo-cho*
*Timecode for scene: 1:17:05 – 1:20:11*

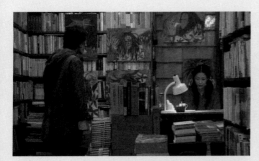 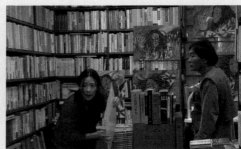

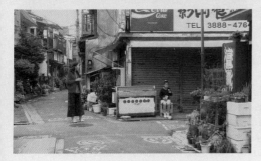 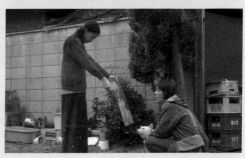

# GUGU THE CAT (2008)

*Inokashira Park, 1-17-6, Gotenyama, Musashino-shi*

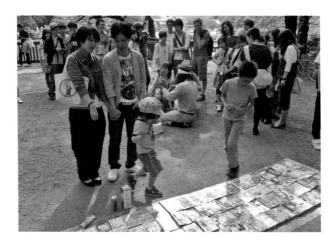

**DON'T MISTAKE *GUGU THE CAT*** for a pet film. Isshin Inudo's film adaptation of Yumiko Oshima's autobiographical manga is about the people in the story, most notably Asako (Kyoko Koizumi), a 40-something cartoonist dealing with loss, illness, and all the other concerns that sneak up on you when you reach middle age. Don't let the rustic setting fool you either. Asako's home is not in a mountain village but a green oasis nestled in Tokyo's Kichijoji, Inokashira Park. The film makes the most of its location, name-checking Sato's fried meatballs and half a dozen other traditions beloved of Kichijoji locals, and setting much of the action in the park's greenery. The lake in the centre of Inokashira is lined with cherry trees, and in *sakura* season the park hosts thousands of picnicking locals. In this sequence Asako chases after GuGu, who has run off. Inudo treats the viewer to a bird's-eye view of the park, then a shot of Asako walking by the lake's fountain – a favorite background for photographers. Soon Seiji (Kase Ryo) is calling to her from a tree above, having retrieved her cat. One tantalizingly brief conversation later and Seiji walks away, leaves in his hair, as Asako gazes after him. In addition to the fountain, footbridge, and swan boats delighting locals and tourists alike, Inokashira has a must-visit destination for anime fans on its border: Hayao Miyazaki's Ghibli Museum. Signs featuring the beloved Totoro character point the way, a short walk from anywhere in the park. ◆*Eric Evans*

(Photo ©www.traveljapanblog.com)

*Directed by Isshin Inudo*
*Scene description: Chasing a cat, finding love in Inokashira Park*
*Timecode for scene: 0:30:38 – 0:34:50*

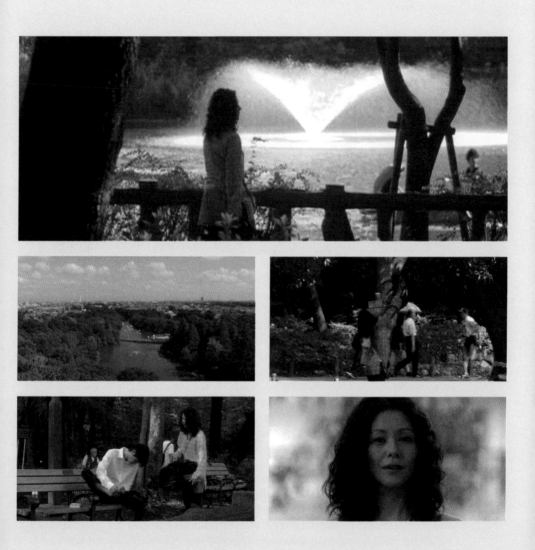

# THE TASTE OF FISH/
# TSUKIJI UOGASHI SANDAIME (2008)

LOCATION *Tsukiji Fish Market*

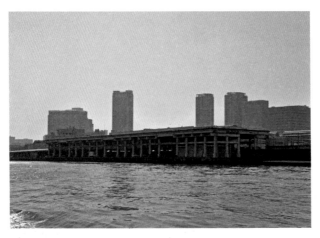
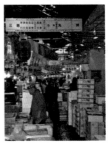

**WHAT HAPPENS WHEN** you see your girlfriend riding her bike across town at an ungodly hour of the morning? In a romantic comedy, you might follow her to the waterfront area just past the Tsukiji Station stop on the Tokyo Metro Hibiya Line only to learn that she's part of a family of fishmongers at world famous Tokyo Metropolitan Central Wholesale Market, better known to tourists as Tsukiji Market. *The Taste of Fish* introduces viewers to this Mecca of seafood via a series of behind-the-scenes shots showing how vast and complicated the world's biggest wholesale fish market really is. The film's unprecedented access reveals a facility no less hectic or high stakes than the New York Stock Exchange. The numbers are staggering: miniature forklifts buzz around a vast delivery area for 900 stalls, 65,000 workers prepare and price over 400 varieties of seafood, and restaurant buyers from around the world shop and bid on the day's catch to the tune of US$5.5 billion each year. Stumbling into the complicated world of Tsukiji Market is low-level businessman Shuntaro (Takao Osawa). His girlfriend Asuka (Rena Tanaka) is working the early a.m. shift to man the fish stall her family has held for generations, while her father Seijiro (Akira Emoto) recuperates from an operation. Shuntaro wants to help but knows nothing about seafood outside of the sushi he orders at business lunches. The viewer learns along with him as he gets a crash course in the taste, and business, of fish. **➻ Eric Evans**

(Photos ©Japon Avril)

*Directed by Shingo Matsubara*
**Scene description: Behind the scenes and between the stalls at Tsukiji Market**
**Timecode for scene: 0:12:36 – 0:13:33**

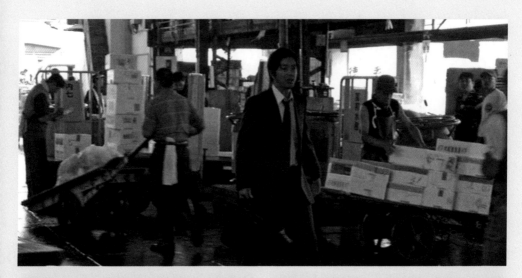

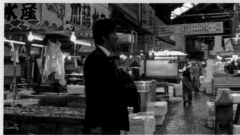 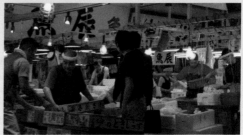

# TOKYO SONATA (2008)

LOCATION *Minato-ku, Tokyo Bay near Sengakuji Temple*

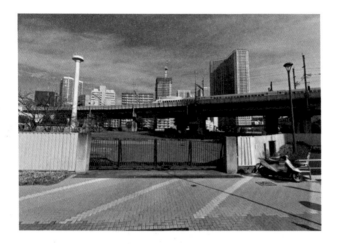

**AFTER RYUHEI SASAKI** (Teruyuki Kagawa) is unceremoniously let go from his long-time office job, he continues the charade of going to work every day in his suit. He's ashamed to reveal the truth to his family. His cash dwindling, Sasaki lowers himself to lining up for handouts of soup with the homeless at a small public rest area nestled among the criss-crossing highway overpasses and train tracks of Tokyo Bay. Sasaki finishes his pathetic meal and notices another salaryman his own age walk past. They make eye contact, unsure whether to engage. Finally the man says 'I thought it was you, Sasaki,' and approaches. It's his old high school classmate, Kurosu. What follows is an incredibly uncomfortable moment where Sasaki can't admit why he's hanging around the dead end patch of brick and cement. Kurosu takes an important business call, radiating success. As the homeless shuffle by, Kurosu eyes the soup line and decides to try some. It's not long before he admits he's unemployed, too. The two old friends sit amidst construction site debris, laughing at the absurdity of their circumstances. Shot at a waterworks facility located in the southern tip of Minato ward on Tokyo Bay's 249 km² of reclaimed land, the scene epitomizes Kurosawa's penchant for filming the lesser-seen side of the megalopolis. Kurosawa has remarked that many of his locations later disappear altogether. A short distance away on the opposite side of busy route 15 is Sengakuji, resting place of Asano Naganori and the 47 Ronin.
**⤚Jason Gray**

*Directed by Kiyoshi Kurosawa*
**Scene description: Sasaki runs into an old classmate in an unlikely place**
**Timecode for scene: 0:18:36 – 0:21:09**

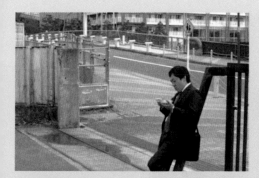
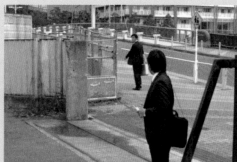
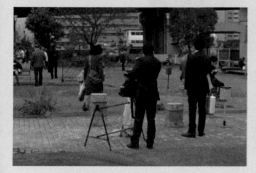
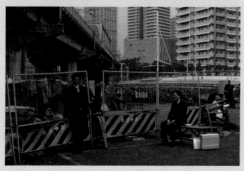

# TOKYO! (SEGMENT 'SHAKING TOKYO') (2008)

LOCATION *Shibuya Crossing*

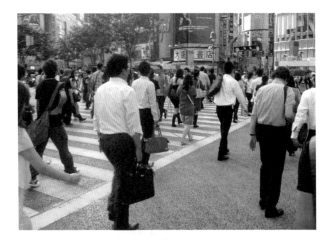

**THOUGH MOSTLY FILMED** in the neighbourhood of Kugayama, Bong Joon-ho's third and final piece in the 2008 *Tokyo!* triptych, 'Shaking Tokyo', features a discreet epiphanic scene at Shibuya's world-famous scramble crossing, where thousands of pedestrians normally flood the intersection. Shot from above, the scene shows the unnamed protagonist (Teruyuki Kagawa) crossing the area, now voided of the usual massive crowds, like a sequence out of a science fiction movie (like the Times Square of *I Am Legend* [Francis Lawrence, 2007] or *Last Man on Earth* ). As the character traverses the screen and the street, a fundamental void suddenly appears and punctures the very heart and fabric of the city, emptied of its blood: the passers-by who pump life into an otherwise absent centre. Something more troubling is also suggested: behind the everyday hustle and bustle of the megalopolis, there is an intrinsic emptiness (much like the Imperial Palace from which the Emperor is absent); a flat line that denies the concrete vertical masses of any meaning. This emptiness appears on different levels that are relevant to the Shibuya Crossing scene: the protagonist is a *hikikomori*, a 'shut-in', one who avoids others and stays inside for years on end: in other words, he is himself is a form of void. Withdrawn within his apartment, he refutes the existence of the exterior world as he stacks pizza boxes in towers strangely reminiscent of the empty verticality of the skyscrapers outside. Paradoxically, this void inhabits and inspires *Shaking Tokyo*'s lyrical radiance and wonderment. **➛Samuel Jamier**

(Photo ©Hakeem Gadi)

*Directed by Bong Joon-ho*
**Scene description: The last man on Earth**
**Timecode for scene: 1:39:13 – 1:39:24**

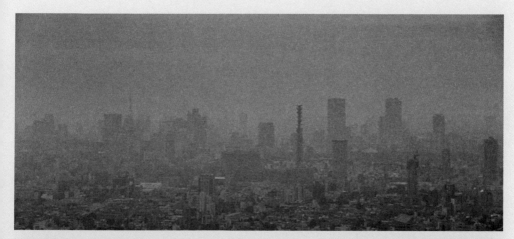

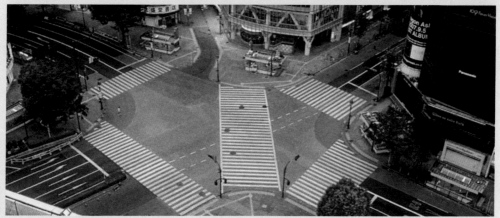

# ENTER THE VOID (2009)

LOCATION *Hotel Rakuen, 2-14-1 Kabukicho, Shinjuku-Ku*

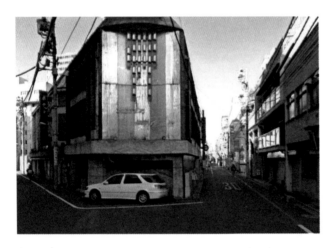

**GASPAR NOÉ'S ENTER THE VOID** is an ultra-sensory cinematic experience that depicts a young drug dealer's demise and subsequent out-of-body journey through the neon-lit nightscapes of Tokyo. Love it or hate it, it is a startling film with Tokyo as a central character. The film is predominantly set in Kabukicho's warren of hostess bars, restaurants, cinemas, massage parlors and love hotels. With complex (and expensively produced) visuals that blend real locations, studio sets and CG, *Enter the Void* seamlessly floats above Kabukicho's myriad rooftops, penetrating walls to spy on human inhabitants gripped by vice, particularly sexual. Much of the film is shot from just behind the head of its protagonist, Oscar (Nathanial Brown). A flashback sequence depicts the lead up to Oscar's fatal drug bust at grimy bar The Void. Oscar's teenaged buyer (and eventual betrayer), Victor, is furious that Oscar has slept with his mother. He smashes him over the head with a bottle and runs off. Oscar takes chase through a dark alley toward the light, emerging at the scene of a police shakedown shot in front of decrepit, abandoned love hotel 'Rakuen' ('Pleasure Garden') – an actual location. He then jogs deeper into love hotel territory, where the garish, art deco sex sanctuaries of today stand, but Victor has already disappeared into the night. The setting prefigures the film's climactic flight through the rooms of a fantastical love hotel. ➥*Jason Gray*

(Photo ©Google street view)

*Directed by Gaspar Noé*
*Scene description: Oscar searches for Victor in the back streets of Kabukicho*
*Timecode for scene: 1:22:40 – 1:25:03*

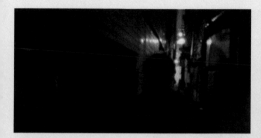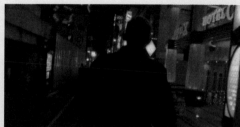

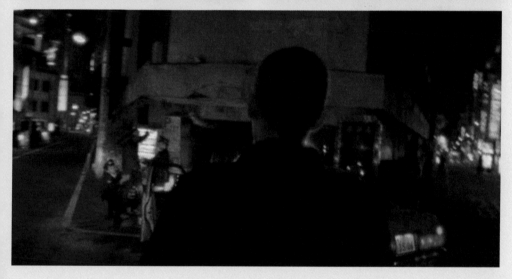

# MAP OF THE SOUNDS OF TOKYO (2009)

*Hotel Bastille, Kabuki-cho, Shinjuku*

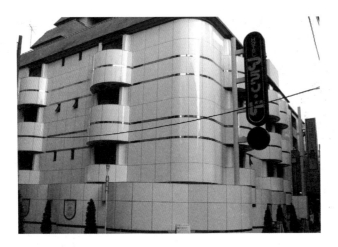

**FOR BACKPACKERS** in small towns in Japan, love hotels offer a great alternative to hostels. If you're a couple, for the same price you can get a big bed, luxury bathroom, and mood-making waterfall artwork. If visiting Tokyo, you can buy yourself a night in a themed fantasy. Isabel Coixet's *Map of the Sounds of Tokyo* might be one of those fantasies. The film features rain swept streets, apartments, and shops that are uncharacteristically spacious, and the cinematography makes the city move with a foreign romanticism. The Japan/Europe dichotomy in the relationship between Ryu and David (Japanese female assassin and *gaijin* target) is also prevalent in the choice of locations in the film, especially in the pivotal scene in Hotel Bastille. Originally a swamp, a duck sanctuary, and then the site of a girl's school, Kabuki-cho is now a Mecca for pleasure-seekers and escapists. Named for a *kabuki* theatre that was never built, it is an area in Shinjuku popular for its many nightclubs, hostess bars, massage parlors and tacky love hotels. The unlikely couple spends the evening here strolling from *ramen* shop to *jazz-kissa*, and end up at the Hotel Bastille in a room called Place des Vosges, named after the largest square in Paris built by Henri IV in 1612. Oddly, the room is decorated like the inside of a train car. Charged with semiotic static, it's the kind of room that would excite Roland Barthes. It is spaces like this that give Tokyo its electricity. **••Naomi Hocura**

**Above** A typical Love hotel in kabuki-cho (Photo ©Chris 73)

*Directed by Isabel Coixet*
**Scene description: A visit to Hotel Bastille**
**Timecode for scene: 0:46:02 – 0:47:27**

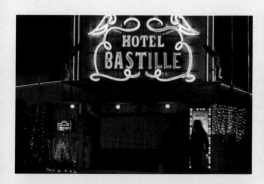
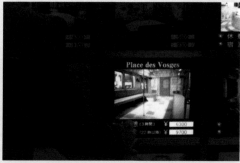
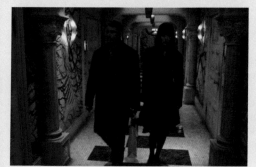
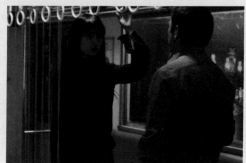

# EDO

*Old Tokyo Resurrected on Film*

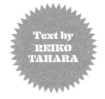

Text by
REIKO
TAHARA

**THE 265-YEAR LONG EDO PERIOD** (1603–1868) is known as an era of peace. The Tokugawa Shogunate enforced this peace through its isolation policy to block Western colonial expansion, and by the 'Alternate Attendance' law requiring *daimyo*, or warlords, across Japan to reside in the capital of Edo every other year. As a result of this policy, major roads were paved across Japan and lodging-towns grew up to meet the needs of the *daimyo* travelling to Edo.

The Edo Period began to crumble with the arrival of American 'Black Ships' in 1853, which forced the opening of Japan. Civil war preceded the re-establishment of the Emperor's power. During the Meiji Restoration, as it is referred to, Edo was renamed Tokyo, men chopped off their topknots, and the political system was modernized under such slogans as 'wealth and military strength' and 'Japanese spirit with Western learning'. Edo, therefore, represents the ripened, last phase of samurai Japan.

After World War II, films containing violence, patriotic thoughts, or ideas of suicide

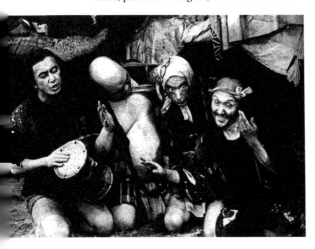

or revenge killing were banned or censored. This included most samurai films. When US censorship was lifted in 1952, there was a surge of *jidai-geki*, or period films, many of which chose the end of the Edo Period as their setting. In *Before Dawn* (Kozaburo Yoshimura, 1953), we don't see Edo; however, its absence makes it more chillingly present. Based on a novel by the same title, it chronicles the tragic life of Hanzo Aoyama (Shin Date), the patriarch of a privileged family in Kiso, a lodging-town between Tokyo and Kyoto, in the turbulent times following the arrival of the Black Ships. Hanzo's family has overseen the village and provided rooms for travelling *daimyo* for generations. Influenced by the new nativist ideas during his study in Edo, Hanzo welcomes the change and believes the restoration will benefit the common people, but the opposite happens and Hanzo's sanity deteriorates. He begs his wife to let him go to Tokyo one last time. There, he secretly makes a direct plea to the Emperor on behalf of the people. Aged and insane Hanzo eventually torches his family's temple and dies in a jail cell. Here Edo/ Tokyo represents the power, the absolute centre, which accommodates the changing rulers but remains unkind to the unfortunate. It is meaningful that *Before Dawn* was made right after the US Occupation ended, leaving many Japanese feeling lost about what to believe in.

*Sun in the Last Days of the Shogunate* (Yuzo Kawashima, 1957) is a comedy classic starring Frankie Sakai as Saheiji, a Shinagawa downtowner in 1862. In the opening sequence, Kawashima directly parallels the chaotic post-war Tokyo with post-Black Ships Edo. In nineteenth-century Shinagawa we see friction between foreigners and locals, then the film jumps to 1950s Shinagawa,

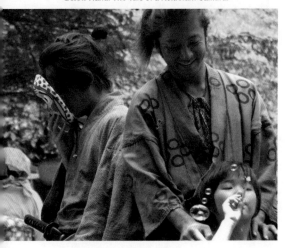

busy with daytime traffic, empty restaurant malls and Japanese 'pan pan' prostitutes with American GIs. Saheiji is the embodiment of the *iki* (chic) of Edo. After a night of treating friends at a brothel, he somehow manages to remain and get a job there. He is smart, swift, kind to prostitutes and quickly gains popularity, but avoids any commitment, even turning down propositions from the top geisha. Film critic Tadao Sato points out that because Edo was the only place where town people could make fun of samurai (since they were mostly country hicks), the *iki* of Edo residents was the counterpoint to the samurai's virtues – loyalty, bravery, respect for authorities, etc. Saheiji's declaration at the end of the film, 'There's no heaven, nor hell. I'm gonna live!' was the cry of all Tokyoites who resiliently survived the hard post-war years.

Shohei Imamura's *Eijanaika* (1981) appeared much later, but inherited the same rebellious spirit of his cinematic master, Yuzo Kawashima. Set in 1867, months preceding the restoration of the Emperor's power, the commoners of Edo revolt using *Eijanaika* ('Why Not?') as their mantra. Imamura tackles this true story of Old Edo head-on by reconstructing the Ryogoku Bridge that divides the 'official Edo' and 'unofficial Edo'. Hundreds of entertainment workers from the East side cross the river via the bridge or by boat to rebel against the official West side of Ryogoku, populated by wealthy merchants and high-ranking samurai. Women from the show-tents lift their kimono and moon the rows of samurai from the West armed with guns. This uprising is eventually brought down with many commoners massacred, but as always Imamura depicts the lower classes with compassion and even admiration with the belief that they can never be defeated.

Akira Kurosawa's curious treatment of Edo shines in *The Lower Depths* (1957). Kurosawa chooses to set his own version of Russian author Maxim Gorky's stage play in the middle of nineteenth-century Edo, a period known for its prosperity and stability. The result is a dark comedy with the tenants of an Edo *nagaya* (dilapidated tenement). A notorious perfectionist Kurosawa, along with his art director Yoshiro Muraki, constructed their present day fictional tenements from actual period specific lumber and props suggesting that people in 'the lower depths' are always with us regardless of borders or time.

It is worth noting that, although samurai have been stereotyped as superhuman, disciplined warriors, there were many *ronin*, or unemployed samurai, living in *nagaya* among commoners in Old Edo. These became beloved characters in many *jidai-gei* – men who don't behave outwardly like samurai, but who often times harbour hidden skills with a sword. *Hana: The Tale of a Reluctant Samurai* (Hirokazu Koreeda, 2006) further breaks this myth of samurai as disciplined strong warriors. Soza (Junichi Okada) is a samurai who came to Edo to avenge the death of his father, but he has no skill in combat and even develops compassion for his foe (Tadanobu Asano). Instead of carrying out bloody vengeance Soza falls in love, not only with a beautiful widow (Rie Miyazawa), but with the modest *nagaya* life. Koreeda views Soza with a documentarian's sensitivity and reminds us that samurai weren't mythical creatures, but the ancestors of today's Japanese. ✦

**It is meaningful that *Before Dawn* was made right after the US Occupation ended leaving many Japanese feeling lost about what to believe in.**

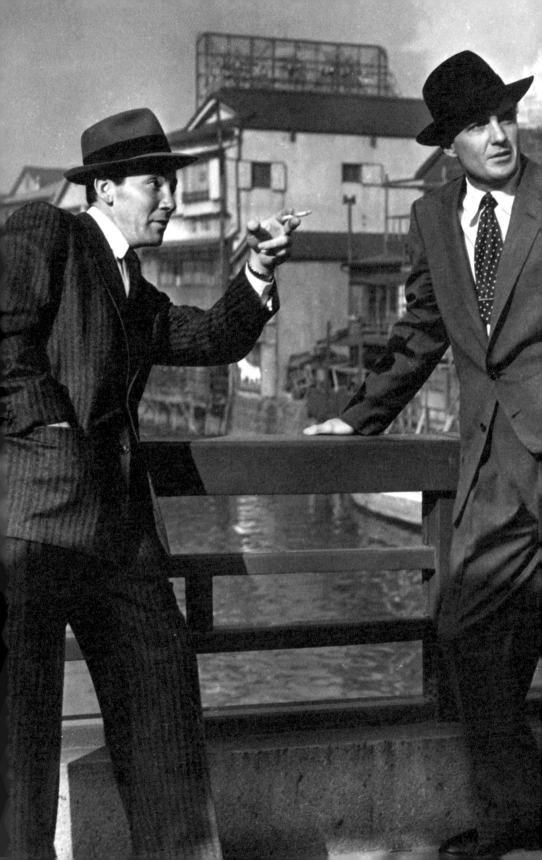

# GO FURTHER

*Recommended reading, useful websites and further viewing*

## BOOKS

**Currents in Japanese Cinema**
By Tadao Sato
(Kodansha America Inc., 1987)

**The Encyclopedia of Japanese Pop Culture**
By Mark Schilling
(Weatherhill, 1997)

**Historical Dictionary of Tokyo**
By Roman Cybriwsky
(The Scarecrow Press, Inc., 2011)

**A Hundred Years of Japanese Film:
A Concise History, with a Selective Guide
to DVDs and Videos**
By Donald Richie
(Kodansha International, 2005)

**Japanese Film Directors**
By Audie Bock
(Kodansha America Inc., 1985)

**The Midnight Eye Guide to New
Japanese Film**
By Tom Mes and Jasper Sharp
(Stone Bridge Press, 2004)

**Tokyo:
A Cultural Guide to Japan's Capital City**
By John H. Martin and Phyllis G. Martin
(Tuttle Publishing, 1996)

**Tokyo A Cultural History (Cityscapes)**
By Stephen Mansfield
(Oxford University Press, 2009)

**Tokyo from Edo to Showa 1867–1989:
The Emergence of the World's Greatest City**
By Edward Seidensticker
(Tuttle Publishing, 2010)

## BOOKS (continued)

**Visions of Japanese Modernity:
Articulations of Cinema, Nation, and
Spectatorship, 1895–1925**
By Aaron Gerow
(University of California Press, 2010)

## ONLINE

**www.japan-guide.com**
Japan-Guide.com

**www.midnighteye.com**
Visions of Japanese Cinema

**http://tinyurl.com/3s3jr9**
M.I.T. Visualizing Cultures

**nishikataeiga.blogspot.com**
Nishikata Film Review

**www.planettokyo.com**
Planet Tokyo

**www.aarongerow.com**
Tangemania: Aaron Gerow's Japanese
Film Page

**www.jfilmpowwow.blogspot.com**
The Toronto J-Film Pow-Wow

**www.vcinemashow.com**
Vcinema

# CONTRIBUTORS

*Editor and contributing writer biographies*

### EDITOR

**CHRIS MAGEE** is the founder and editor of the *Toronto J-Film Pow-Wow*, the premiere Japanese film blog in Canada. He is also the co-programmer and co-artistic director of the 'Shinsedai Cinema Festival', a showcase of new and independent film from Japan that takes place annually at the Japanese Canadian Cultural Centre in Toronto. Chris has also guest curated and lectured on Japanese film in North America and Europe, and has been responsible for premiering the films of experimental film-makers Masaki Iwana and Kanai Katsu in Canada. He has contributed to online film publications such as *Midnight Eye*, and his latest project was curating a programme of rare Butoh dance films featuring Tatsumi Hijikata and Kazuo Ohno for the 2011 'CanAsian International Dance Festival'.

### CONTRIBUTORS

**JACOPO FRANCESCO ACQUA** is a Ph.D. candidate at Ca' Foscari University of Venice. He graduated from Ca' Foscari University in 2005, with a dissertation on movie adaptations of Japanese literature concerning the *burakumin* issue. During his undergraduate years at Ca' Foscari he developed a strong interest in studying the portrayal of minorities in Japanese cinema; after spending two years at Meiji Gakuin Daigaku in Tokyo sponsored by the Monbukagakusho scholarship, he is now conducting a research about depictions of gay and lesbian characters on screen. He assists the 'Venice International Film Festival' and 'Torino Film Festival' staff as Japanese/Italian interpreter, and also works as web editor for two university-related websites *asiamedia.unive.it* and *cafoscaricinema.unive.it*.

**MATTEO BOSCAROL** is an Italian film critic based in Japan, who mainly writes for the newspaper *Il Manifesto* and the cinema website *Cineclandestino.it*. He has contributed essays on Japanese directors such as Nagisa Oshima, Satoshi Kon, Shinya Tsukamoto and Yoshihiko Matsui to several periodicals and volumes. He also has edited a volume of William S. Burroughs interviews and is doing independent research on Butoh/Cinema, and the connections between Deleuze and Guattari and Japan. He is currently working on a monograph about the Japanese actor Tadanobu Asano.

**JOHN BERRA** is a Professor of Film Studies at Nanjing University. He is the author of *Declarations of Independence: American Cinema and the Partiality of Independent Production* (2008) and the editor of the *Directory of World Cinema: American Independent* (2010) and the *Directory of World Cinema: Japan* (2010). John has also contributed chapters to *The End: An Electric Sheep Anthology* (2011) and *The Companion to Film Noir* (2012), while his film criticism has appeared in *Electric Sheep*, *Film International*, *The Big Picture* and *VCinema*.

**ERIC EVANS** is a creative director specializing in magazine and direct mail content. In his free time he enjoys travel, photography, diving and (especially) watching Asian films. He writes about those films for the *Toronto J-Film Pow-Wow*, *VCinema* and whoever else will have him. He currently lives in Portland, Oregon, USA with his wife and dog.

**JASON GRAY** has been based in Japan for ten years and works in the film industry as a journalist, consultant and professional translator for Japanese movies and film festivals. He is the Japan correspondent for global film industry journal *Screen International* and has written on cinema for publications and websites including *The Japan Times*, *CNNGo* and *Midnight Eye*. Among his translation and consultation clients are Toei, Tokyo Broadcast System, Nippon Television, Avex Entertainment, Asmik Ace, Gaga Communications, Tokyo International Film Festival, Tokyo FILMeX, Skip City International D-Cinema Festival, and individual film directors and producers including Kiyoshi Kurosawa and Sabu. Selected works include *Tomorrow's Joe* (Fumihiko Sori), *Troubleman* (Sabu) and *K-20: The Legend of the Black Mask* (Shimako Sato). He is currently focusing on screenwriting and producing. He is serving as an associate producer on upcoming Max Mannix project *Yellow Earth*.

**MATTHEW HARDSTAFF**, born in England and raised in Canada, is a Toronto-based writer, film-maker and dungeon master who is a regular contributor to the *Toronto J-Film Pow-Wow* and is currently working on his first feature film, *Bluebird*. Whilst he has a very diverse taste in films, his deepest love is that of martial arts and horror. Especially anything ninja oriented.

**JAMES HERON** lived in Japan for eleven years, working as a teacher, administrator and translator. As executive director of the Japanese Canadian Cultural Centre in Toronto since 2000, he has hosted visits by Their Majesties The Emperor and Empress of Japan, Princess Takamado, and many leading Japanese artists, politician and business people. He is president of the Chado Urasenke Tankokai Tea Society in Toronto and the Executive Director of the 'Shinsedai Cinema Festival'. James has a second *dan* in kendo.

**BRANDON HOCURA** is a musician, producer and writer living in Toronto. He has an academic background in film and art history, and spent four years in Tokyo immersing himself in Japanese art, music and culture. He is co-founder of Polyphasic Recordings, a label and studio that focuses on electronic and experimental music. Currently Brandon is member of the psychedelic pop group VOWLS and DJs, edits and remixes under the name Grand AM.

**NAOMI HOCURA** does a lot of things; some real, some imaginary. While living in Tokyo for four years she developed a taste for the under-represented under-belly of Japanese art and culture, and now presents film and art events in Toronto under the name ANGURA! (angura.org). Her recent projects include *Seconds Under the Sun*, a night of short Japanese animation that screened in various Canadian cities between August 2009 and August 2010, and a live soundtrack performance with her band VOWLS to Kenji Mizoguchi's *The Water Magician* at the 2010 'Shinsedai Cinema Festival'. As a day job she experiments with sonic-aromatherapy for her home spa product line SPA KOSMISCHE.

**CATHERINE MUNROE HOTES** is a Canadian freelance film and literary critic and author of the blog *Nishikata Film Review*. She has a doctorate in film and visual culture from the University of Exeter. Her dissertation explored the influence of the cinema of such

# CONTRIBUTORS

directors as Godard, Dreyer and Cocteau on the poetry of Adrienne Rich. She is currently writing a book on Japanese art animation.

**SAMUEL JAMIER** is of Korean descent and grew up in Brittany, France. He graduated from the Ecole Normale Supérieure, Paris, studied at King's College, London, Tokyo University, and at the Sorbonne Nouvelle University. Jamier has been Senior Film Programmer at Japan Society since September 2009. Prior to this, he created 'Live House Korea', a traditional Korean performing arts program for The Korea Society, and co-programmed the 2007 'New York Korean Film Festival'. Since, he has programmed *The Double-Edged Sword: The Chambara Films of Shintaro Katsu & Raizo Ichikawa* in collaboration with Chris D. (Desjardins), and curated *Zen and Its Opposite: Essential (& Turbulent) Japanese Arthouse*; *Run, Salaryman, Run: A Retrospective of Sabu's Films*; *Shadows of the Rising Sun: Cinema and Empire*; *Japan Cuts 2010*, and the Globus Film Series: *Mad, Bad.... & Dangerous to Know: Three Untamed Beauties* and *Hardest Men in Town: Yakuza Chronicles of Sin, Sex & Violence*.

**JON JUNG** is a language educator who lives in the San Francisco Bay Area. He is a veteran of independent, DIY media and has worked in college radio, started and contributed to various underground 'zines covering music, film and photography and even had his own record label featuring Japanese punk bands. He is the founder of VCinema (Vcinemashow. com), a website and bi-weekly podcast that covers Asian cinema from cult to the classics and works as its producer and editor-in-chief. Jon lived in Tokyo for six years and, besides

his interest in the film and music of Japan, his main fields of study and research include cultural anthropology and linguistics, in particular the indigenous languages of Japan, its language policy and language shift.

**TOM MES** is the author of *Agitator: The Cinema of Takashi Miike* and *Iron Man: The Cinema of Shinya Tsukamoto* (FAB Press), as well as the founder and editor-in-chief of the authoritative website on Japanese film, MidnightEye.com. A contributor to *Film Comment*, *Rue Morgue* and *De Filmkrant* among others, Tom also co-wrote *The Midnight Eye Guide to New Japanese Film* with Jasper Sharp (Stone Bridge Press), and *Tokyolife: Art and Design* with Ian Luna, Jasper Sharp, et al. (Rizzoli International). With Anna Harrison, he translated *Cinema and the Shoah* (SUNY Press) from the original French volume published by Cahiers du Cinéma.

**MARIA ROBERTA NOVIELLI** specialized in Japanese cinema at the Nihon University, Tokyo, and now teaches Japanese Cinema and Literature at the Department of Philosophy and Cultural Heritage at the University Ca' Foscari, Venice. She is a contributor to numerous Italian magazines and the author of *Storia del cinema giapponese* (History of Japanese Cinema, Marsilio, 2001), the first history of Japanese cinema written in Italy, and of *Metamorfosi – Schegge di violenza nel nuovo cinema giapponese* (Metamorphosis - Splinters of Violence in the New Japanese Cinema, Epika, 2010). In addition, she has co-operated with various Italian film festivals, organizing retrospectives on Japanese film directors and is Chair of the press conferences related to Japanese films for the 'Venice

Film Festival'. She is also the chief editor of *AsiaMedia*, the Italian website which focuses on Asian cinema, and editor of the book series *Schemi Orientali* – Editrice Cafoscarina – Venezia. She is also the Rector's delegate for all the activities of Ca' Foscari Cinema, including the 'Ca' Foscari Short Film Festival'.

**MARC SAINT-CYR** is a staff writer for the blog the *Toronto J-Film Pow-Wow*. He has also contributed to such online film publications as *Midnight Eye*, *Row Three* and the first and second volumes of the *Directory of World Cinema: Japan* (Intellect Ltd). Marc also runs his own blog, *Subtitle Literate*. He holds a special interest in Asian and European cinemas.

**STEPHEN SARRAZIN** is an art and film critic, professor and visual artist who splits his time between Tokyo and Paris. Not only does Sarrazin write for Cahiers du Cinema and teach part-time at the Tokyo University of the Arts, but he has had his photographs exhibited alongside the work of film director Katsuhito Ishii at the Galerie Vanessa Quang in Paris and played a lead role in Shinya Tsukamoto's 2010 film *Tetsuo the Bullet Man*.

**REIKO TAHARA** is a film-maker who grew up in Tokyo and has lived in New York for twenty years. Her films have been exhibited at festivals and art venues worldwide. She collaborates with film-maker/composer Max Uesugi and their latest creative documentary, *The GateKeeper of Enmyoin: According to a 95-year-old Female Buddhist Priest*, is scheduled to open in Tokyo in summer 2011. Reiko is a recipient of Japanese Government Emerging Artists Overseas Fellowship, and co-recipient of production grants from National Endowment for the Arts, Jerome Foundation and the Japan-US Friendship Commissions, among others. She currently teaches at NYU, and has taught Japanese cinema, documentary history, film production and fundraising at Temple University, Hunter College, New School, and City College of New York. Max and Reiko run the Uno Port Art Films, an annual summer film series in Okayama, Japan. Her writing regularly appears on *Webdice* published by Uplink Theatre in Shibuya, Tokyo.

# FILMOGRAPHY

*A comprehensive list of all films mentioned or featured*

| | |
|---|---|
| About Love, Tokyo (1992) | 79 |
| Adrift in Tokyo (2007) | 6,81,96 |
| Akira (1988) | 42,43,78 |
| All Under the Moon (1993) | 78 |
| Always: Sunset on Third Street (2005) | 5,63,76 |
| Atlanta Boogie (1996) | 78 |
| Babel (2006) | 81,90 |
| Battle Royale (2000) | 6 |
| Before Dawn (1953) | 120 |
| Blade Runner (1982) | 6,106 |
| Blood and Bones (2004) | 78 |
| Breathless (1960) | 98 |
| Bubblegum Crisis (1987) | 43 |
| Burmese Harp, The (1956) | 24 |
| Buy a Suit (2008) | 101,104 |
| Café Lumiere (2003) | 63,66 |
| Code Geass (2006) | 43 |
| Confessions of a Dog (2006) | 5,81,86 |
| Darker Than Black (2007) | 43 |
| Dead or Alive (1999) | 45,56 |
| Death by Hanging (1968) | 78 |
| Demon City Shinjuku (1998) | 43 |
| Diary of a Shinjuku Thief (1969) | 27,32,98,99 |
| Empire of the Senses (1976) | 98 |
| Enlighnment Guaranteed (1999) | 5,63,65 |
| Enter the Void (2009) | 6,101,116 |
| Fast and The Furious: Tokyo Drift, The (2006) | 6 |
| Fear and Trembling (2003) | 63,68 |
| Eijanaika (1981) | 121 |
| Fine, Totally Fine (2008) | 101,107 |
| Ghost in the Shell (1995) | 43 |
| Godzilla/Gojira (1954) | 6,9,18,25 |
| Good Morning (1959) | 61 |
| Gugu the Cat (2008) | 101,108 |
| Hachi: A Dogs Tale (2009) | 52 |
| Hachiko Monogatari (1987) | 45,52 |
| Hana: The Tale of a Reluctant Samuri (2006) | 121 |
| Hidden Blade, The (2004) | 24 |
| House of Bamboo (1955) | 9,20 |
| I Am Legend (2007) | 114 |
| I Was Born, But... (1932) | 61 |
| If You Were Young: Rage (1970) | 5,27,36 |
| Inn in Tokyo (1935) | 60 |
| It's Only Talk/ Yawarakai Seikatsu (2006) | 81,88 |
| It's Tough Being a Man/Tora San (1969) | 5,27,34 |
| Jigoku (1953) | 24 |
| Junk Food (1997) | 79 |
| Kabei: Our Mother (2008) | 24,25 |
| Kakera (2009) | 6 |
| Kikujiro (1999) | 45,58 |

| | |
|---|---|
| Kill Bill Volume I (2003) | 63, 70 |
| Knobody Knows (2004) | 5,63,74 |
| La Jetee (1962) | 48 |
| Last Man on Earth (1964) | 114 |
| Lost In Translation (2003) | 5,63,72 |
| Lower Depths, The (1957) | 121 |
| Map of the Sounds of Tokyo (2009) | 101,118 |
| Millennium Actress (2001) | 43 |
| Nana (2005) | 81,82 |
| Night of the Felines (1972) | 98 |
| Nineteen Year Old Map (1979) | 45,46 |
| Neon Genesis Evangelion (1995) | 43 |
| Norwegian Wood (2010) | 79 |
| Nuance (2006) | 81,92 |
| Only Son, The (1936) | 60 |
| Passing Fancy (1933) | 61 |
| Pom Poko (1994) | 45,54 |
| RahXephon (2007) | 43 |
| Rebuild of Evangelion (2007) | 43 |
| Record of a Tenement Gentleman (1947) | 25 |
| Retribution (2006) | 81,94 |
| Samurai: The Legend of Musashi (1954) | 24 |
| Sana Soleil (1983) | 45,48 |
| Shallowtail Butterfly (1996) | 78 |
| Shin Megami Tensei (1997) | 42 |
| Shinjuku Triad Society (1995) | 99 |
| Stray Dog/Nora Inu (1953) | 9,12,25 |
| Sun in the Last Days of the Shogunate (1957) | 120 |
| Sword of Penitence, The (1927) | 60 |
| Taste of Fish, The (2008) | 101,110 |
| Throw Away Your Books and Rally... (1971) | 27,38,99 |
| Tokyo! (2008) | 101,114 |
| Tokyo-Ga (1985) | 45,50 |
| Tokyo Magnitude 8.0 | 42,43 |
| Tokyo March (1929) | 9,10 |
| Tokyo Olympiad (1965) | 27,28 |
| Tokyo Sonata (2008) | 101,112 |
| Tokyo Story (1953) | 5,9,14,60,61 |
| Tokyo Twilight (1957) | 61 |
| Train Man/Desha Otoko (2005) | 81,84 |
| Twilight Samuri (2002) | 24 |
| When a Woman Ascends the Stairs (1960) | 9,22 |
| Where Chimneys Are Seen (1953) | 9, 16 |
| Where Hot Tears Overflow (1992) | 79 |
| Woman of Tokyo (1933) | 60 |
| World Apartment Horror (1991) | 78 |
| Yakuza, The (1974) | 27,40 |
| Yasukuni (2007) | 101,102 |
| You Only Live Twice (1967) | 27,30 |